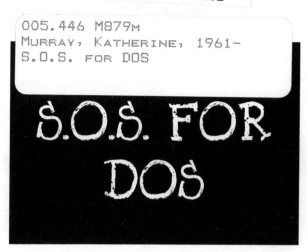

S.O.S. FOR DOS

by Katherine Murray

IDG Books Worldwide, Inc.
An International Data Group Company

San Mateo, California ✦ Indianapolis, Indiana ✦ Boston, Massachusetts

S.O.S. For DOS

Published by

IDG Books Worldwide, Inc.

An International Data Group Company

155 Bovet Road, Suite 310

San Mateo, CA 94402

Library of Congress Catalog Card No.:   93-61313

ISBN: 1-56884-043-8

Printed in the United States of America

10 9 8 7 6 5 4 3 2 1

Distributed in the United States by IDG Books Worldwide, Inc.

Distributed in Canada by Macmillan of Canada, a Division of Canada Publishing Corporation; by Computer and Technical Books in Miami, Florida, for South America and the Caribbean; by Longman Singapore in Singapore, Malaysia, Thailand, and Korea; by Toppan Co. Ltd. in Japan; by Asia Computerworld in Hong Kong; by Woodslane Pty. Ltd. in Australia and New Zealand; and by Transword Publishers Ltd. in the U.K. and Europe.

For information on where to purchase IDG Books outside the U.S., contact Christina Turner at 415-312-0633.

For information on translations, contact Marc Jeffrey Mikulich, Foreign Rights Manager, at IDG Books Worldwide; FAX NUMBER 415-358-1260.

Acknowledgments

Like life, book publishing can be a wonderful, creative, grueling, and rewarding process. This particular book had it all. Thanks to these people who helped make this book what it is:

David Solomon, Publisher, for his initial vision and steadfast eye-on-the-horizon throughout this project. (Rumor has it he's Lao Tsu reincarnated.)

Laurie Smith, Project Editor, for an incredible super-human effort in pulling a variety of elements together and for her patience while trying to teach an old dog new tricks.

Christopher Rozzi, Illustrator, for his *unbelievably* perfect illustrations, and John Kaufeld, Technical Editor and Consulting Writer, for lots of good ideas and the wealth of technical information he provided.

Julie King and Chuck A. Hutchinson for their unfailing and unflagging attention to detail.

My agent, Claudette Moore, for being so gosh-darn good at everything (and a great friend besides).

The team of witch doctors (actual MIS Support Specialists) that we lassoed from Boehringer Mannheim Corporation — Brenda Dalton, Brian W. Eakle, Marti Icenogle, John Kaufeld, Brian J. Raby, and Anna M. Shaw — for the perspective they were able to provide and the gazillion helpful tips we've incorporated.

Beth Jenkins and Accent Technical Communications and Bill Hartman for their unrelenting pursuit of the ultimate design, and Marta Partington, for her helpful hints on the layout. Valery Bourke and Gina Scott for scanning in far more illustrations than most computer books should have.

John Kilcullen, Janna Custer, Brandon Nordin, Polly Papsadore, Marian Bernstein, and the other San Mateo folks for all of their support. Mary Bednarek, Tricia Reynolds, Cindy Phipps, and the other Indianapolis folks for their support. And special thanks to Diane Steele for being the editorial mentor (and moral support) that helped this project to actually get off the ground.

My family — Doug, Kelly, Christopher, and Cameron — for knowing and understanding and being Used To It, and

Kibbles and bits to Simon, who better stop leaving presents in my office or he's cat food.

Katherine Murray

(The publisher would like to give special thanks to Patrick J. McGovern, without whom this book would not have been possible.)

About IDG Books Worldwide

Welcome to the world of IDG Books Worldwide.

IDG Books Worldwide, Inc., is a division of International Data Group, the world's largest publisher of computer-related information and the leading global provider of information services on information technology. IDG publishes over 194 computer publications in 62 countries. Forty million people read one or more IDG publications each month.

If you use personal computers, IDG Books is committed to publishing quality books that meet your needs. We rely on our extensive network of publications, including such leading periodicals as *Macworld, InfoWorld, PC World, Computerworld, Publish, Network World,* and *SunWorld,* to help us make informed and timely decisions in creating useful computer books that meet your needs.

Every IDG book strives to bring extra value and skill-building instruction to the reader. Our books are written by experts, with the backing of IDG periodicals, and with careful thought devoted to issues such as audience, interior design, use of icons, and illustrations. Our editorial staff is a careful mix of high-tech journalists and experienced book people. Our close contact with the makers of computer products helps ensure accuracy and thorough coverage. Our heavy use of personal computers at every step in production means we can deliver books in the most timely manner.

We are delivering books of high quality at competitive prices on topics customers want. At IDG, we believe in quality, and we have been delivering quality for over 25 years. You'll find no better book on a subject than an IDG book.

John Kilcullen
President and C.E.O.
IDG Books Worldwide, Inc.

IDG Books Worldwide, Inc. is a division of International Data Group. The officers are Patrick J. McGovern, Founder and Board Chairman; Walter Boyd, President. International Data Group's publications include: ARGENTINA's Computerworld Argentina, InfoWorld Argentina; ASIA's Computerworld Hong Kong, PC World Hong Kong, Computerworld Southeast Asia, PC World Singapore, Computerworld Malaysia, PC World Malaysia; AUSTRALIA's Computerworld Australia, Australian PC World, Australian Macworld, Network World, Reseller, IDG Sources; AUSTRIA's Computerwelt Oesterreich, PC Test; BRAZIL's Computerworld, Mundo IBM, Mundo Unix, PC World, Publish; BULGARIA's Computerworld Bulgaria, Ediworld, PC & Mac World Bulgaria; CANADA's Direct Access, Graduate Computerworld, InfoCanada, Network World Canada; CHILE's Computerworld, Informatica; COLOMBIA's Computerworld Colombia; CZECH REPUBLIC's Computerworld, Elektronika, PC World; DENMARK's CAD/CAM WORLD, Communications World, Computerworld Danmark, LOTUS World, Macintosh Produktkatalog, Macworld Danmark, PC World Danmark, PC World Produktguide, Windows World; EQUADOR's PC World; EGYPT's Computerworld (CW) Middle East, PC World Middle East; FINLAND's MikroPC, Tietoviikko, Tietoverkko; FRANCE's Distributique, GOLDEN MAC, InfoPC, Languages & Systems, Le Guide du Monde Informatique, Le Monde Informatique, Telecoms & Reseaux; GERMANY's Computerwoche, Computerwoche Focus, Computerwoche Extra, Computerwoche Karriere, Information Management, Macwelt, Netzwelt, PC Welt, PC Woche, Publish, Unit; HUNGARY's Alaplap, Computerworld SZT, PC World, ; INDIA's Computers & Communications; ISRAEL's Computerworld Israel, PC World Israel; ITALY's Computerworld Italia, Lotus Magazine, Macworld Italia, Networking Italia, PC World Italia; JAPAN's Computerworld Japan, Macworld Japan, SunWorld Japan, Windows World; KENYA's East African Computer News; KOREA's Computerworld Korea, Macworld Korea, PC World Korea; MEXICO's Compu Edicion, Compu Manufactura, Computacion/Punto de Venta, Computerworld Mexico, MacWorld, Mundo Unix, PC World, Windows; THE NETHERLAND'S Computer! Totaal, LAN Magazine, MacWorld; NEW ZEALAND's Computer Listings, Computerworld New Zealand, New Zealand PC World; NIGERIA's PC World Africa; NORWAY's Computerworld Norge, C/World, Lotusworld Norge, Macworld Norge, Networld, PC World Ekspress, PC World Norge, PC World's Product Guide, Publish World, Student Data, Unix World, Windowsworld, IDG Direct Response; PANAMA's PC World; PERU's Computerworld Peru, PC World; PEOPLES REPUBLIC OF CHINA's China Computerworld, PC World China, Electronics International, China Network World; IDG HIGH TECH BEIJING's New Product World; IDG SHENZHEN's Computer News Digest; PHILLIPPINES' Computerworld, PC World; POLAND's Computerworld Poland, PC World/Komputer; PORTUGAL's Cerebro/PC World, Correio Informatico/Computerworld, MacIn; ROMANIA's PC World; RUSSIA's Computerworld-Moscow, Mir-PC, Sety; SLOVENIA's Monitor Magazine; SOUTH AFRICA's Computing S.A.; SPAIN's Amiga World, Computerworld Espana, Communicaciones World, Macworld Espana, NeXTWORLD, PC World Espana, Publish, Sunworld; SWEDEN's Attack, ComputerSweden, Corporate Computing, Lokala Natverk/LAN, Lotus World, MAC&PC, Macworld, Mikrodatorn, PC World, Publishing & Design (CAP), Datalngenjoren, Maxi Data, Windows World; SWITZERLAND's Computerworld Schweiz, Macworld Schweiz, PC & Workstation; TAIWAN's Computerworld Taiwan, Global Computer Express, PC World Taiwan; THAILAND's Thai Computerworld; TURKEY's Computerworld Monitor, Macworld Turkiye, PC World Turkiye; UNITED KINGDOM's Lotus Magazine, Macworld, Sunworld; UNITED STATES' AmigaWorld, Cable in the Classroom, CD Review, CIO, Computerworld, Desktop Video World, DOS Resource Guide, Electronic News, Federal Computer Week, Federal Integrator, GamePro, IDG Books, InfoWorld, InfoWorld Direct, Laser Event, Macworld, Multimedia World, Network World, NeXTWORLD, PC Games, PC Letter, PC World Publish; Sumeria, SunWorld, SWATPce, Video Event; VENEZUELA's Computerworld Venezuela, MicroComputerworld Venezuela; VIETNAM's PC World Vietnam

About the author

Although Katherine Murray's first love is her family of three kids and a husband, her other loves include writing, desktop publishing, and computers. With four PCs and a brand-new Macintosh, she has plenty of hardware to indulge her techie passions. After beginning her career in computer book publishing as a copy editor, she eventually graduated to developmental editor. "Then when I was 27-years-old," she says, "I woke up one day and thought, why don't I just do my own computer books? After all, I'd been teaching authors how to write for years." Six years and 30 computer books later, Kathy is now an established author. She enjoys writing the S.O.S. series because it gives her an opportunity to combine humor and creativity in her work. Kathy also enjoys other types of writing and has had articles published in several national magazines.

About the illustrator

Christoper Rozzi has illustrated several computer books in his free time, when he's not wearing his other hat as an indispensible exhibit artist at the Children's Museum in Indianapolis. He somehow managed to find the time to get married during this project, which was amazing because we kept him busy illustrating every hour of the day and night. Chris is an avid comic book collector, and he enjoys scuba diving, hiking, relaxing with his wife, Susan, and deciphering the various personalities of Lagniappe, their cat.

Credits

Publisher
David Solomon

Acquisitions Editor
Janna Custer

Managing Editor
Mary Bednarek

Project Editor
Laurie Ann Smith

Illustrator
Christopher Rozzi

Consulting Writer
John Kaufeld

Editor
Julie King

Editorial Assistant
Patricia R. Reynolds

Technical Reviewer
John Kaufeld

Production Manager
Beth Jenkins

Production Coordinator
Cindy L. Phipps

Production Department
Valery Bourke
Gina Scott

Proofreader
Charles A. Hutchinson

Indexer
Sharon Hilgenberg

Book Design and Production
Beth Jenkins
Accent Technical
  Communications
Bill Hartman

Consultants
Brenda Dalton
Brian W. Eakle
Marti Icenosle
John Kaufeld
Brian J. Raby
Anna M. Shaw

Table of Contents

Prologue

Everything is going just fine. Nice cruise heading down along the coast of Santa Barbara. Before you know it, you'll be in Cancun. Ahhh. Beautiful day. . .
Then it hits. The worst storm in recent history. Lightning. Thunder. Crashing waves. The ship is thrashing about. You can't hang on anymore. Finally, you go over the edge. . . .

FORMAT
Fail
invalid
MANUAL
DIR
RAM
A:
System
DOS
3.5
icon
reboot
Density
delete
Bad Command
F3
error
invalid directory
ABORT
data
Directory
DISKETTE
drive
C>
5.25
Start up
A
prompt
memory
File
BACKUP
Retry
MB
B:

You have been set adrift in a sea of technology. Oh, sure, they gave you a few provisions — a personal computer, a few disks, and, if you're lucky, a soggy manual or two — but then they cut you loose to find your way through a wild world of computing tasks.

The fact that you're out there alone (and that your backside is particularly tempting for passing sharks) doesn't even occur to you until —

Beep. Or **clunk**.

Or `Abort, Retry, Fail?`

Oh, rats, now what? Who can you call? The technical support guy sees you coming and ducks into the rest room. The software trainer does the old sorry-I-can't-help-but-I'm-on-the-phone bit when you walk up. (Funny, you didn't hear the phone ring. . . .)

So there you are. Stranded. With an ornery computer and an operating system uprising beginning to brew.

It's a DOS-eat-disk world, and your data's on the lunch menu.

Welcome to S.O.S. For DOS

Want to get that error fixed so that you can get out of the office and go home? Leaf through these pages a bit. It's in here. *S.O.S. For DOS* includes quick, easy-to-find answers for those problems no one wants to help you with (or you're too embarrassed to ask).

"What?" you may be thinking. "A nontraditional guide to troubleshooting DOS?" After the initial response (which is "What did you expect from IDG?"), I'd have to answer that yes, you've discovered an alternative method of DOS wrangling.

S.O.S. For DOS approaches the trials and tribulations you may face from a fix-it-fast perspective. You won't find lengthy descriptions of complicated batch files (those have something to do with cookies, right?), and you won't hear a lot of gobbledygook about memory management and disk caches (huh?). Let's just deal with the problem and get on with it.

Clear enough.

Navigating through the Book

There are an infinite number of ways to use this book. The most obvious use, of course, is to read it in the manner that suits you best. You may find it helpful to use as a reference: Identify the problem, look it up in the table of contents or the index, and go right to that point in the book. For example, if you've got a disk being chewed up in drive A, turn to Chapter 3, "Disk Difficulties," to find potential solutions (or at least a Band-Aid or two).

If you prefer, you can read the book front to back. That could be inviting danger, however. (Sometimes it's better not to know what *could* happen. . .) If you do, though, you'll find an interesting story to follow in some of the illustrations. You'll also find the following world of sidebars that have themes of their own:

Techie Terms	Definitions of the most appalling computerese
Witch Doctors	How to deal with technical support masters
Satchels	Recipes for making stuff to put in your satchel so that you'll be better prepared in the future
Stepping Stones	Summarized steps for possible solutions

Smoke Signals	Error messages discussed nearby in the chapter
Words of Wisdom	Moral-of-the-story-type teachings from the witch doctor's own experience with DOS and life
Road signs	Warnings and directions to help you find your way
Scrolls	Hints about general troubleshooting adages that all of the best witch doctors already know

When you're in a hurry, sidestep all of these sidebars and go straight to the nitty-gritty problem/solution stuff in the text.

When you're not in hurry — you know, when you're curled up on the couch with your favorite computer book just reading during the commercials — look at the pictures. That is, follow the journey of one lost soul as he tries to survive in a land of confusion.

When You First Encounter DOS

Using DOS for the first time is one of those experiences that you dread for years and then look back on and say, "It really wasn't that bad, was it?" Kind of like driver's ed. Or the junior prom.

When you're just getting started with DOS, it helps to keep things in perspective. You've been thrust into a totally foreign environment — don't expect yourself to cope with everything perfectly.

Lose your cool if that's your style. Direct and honest screaming (preferably at something inanimate) never hurt anything. It may even burn off a few calories.

Or, if you're decidedly passive-aggressive, keep it all inside like the nuns taught you and then rip your DOS book to shreds when no one is looking.

Swim for It!

Hey, look! There's an island in the distance! You'll have to swim for it. Who knows what's over there? Unfriendly natives — cannibals, maybe. And lots of things that go *beep* in the night. And **clunk**. And Abort, Retry, Fail? But there's no turning back now.

You're in luck though — help is on the way because you've already got your *S.O.S. For DOS*.

Part 1

What Happened?
Where Am I?

You've been floating around for who knows how many hours when suddenly there it is — Land! You can barely see an island in the distance. You have to go for it. Cold, bedraggled, exhausted, you finally arrive at the shore. Looks like a friendly enough place. But who could guess the dangers that lie before you.

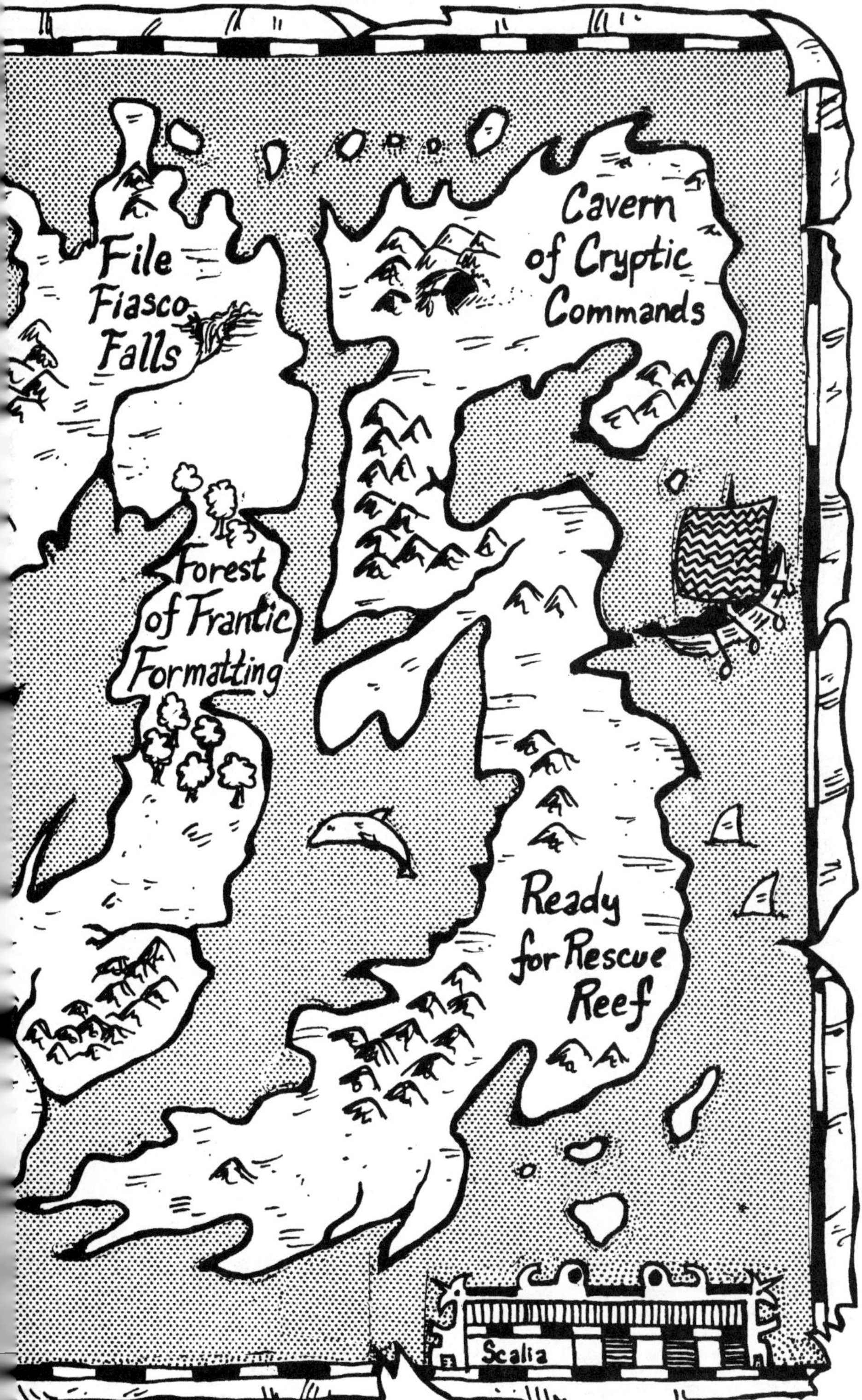
File Fiasco Falls
Cavern of Cryptic Commands
Forest of Frantic Formatting
Ready for Rescue Reef
Scalia

Chapter 1

Problems from the Get-Go

Paths through Peril

Made it to the beach, did you? Nothing too dangerous here, except for a few hungry-looking sand crabs and something with red eyes peering at you from behind a rock. This chapter covers the mysterious *somethings* that might happen as you power up your computer and try to begin your work session. It's pretty rough terrain, so I suggest that you tread (or type) lightly.

At Startup, My Computer Doesn't

Poison: A dead computer

It's your worst nightmare — you reach around, flip that power switch, and . . . nothing. Not a flicker, not a beep. No sign of life at all. What's wrong?

Antidote:

- **Is it plugged in?** And, if it's plugged into a surge protector, is the surge protector plugged into the wall and turned on? The same goes for a UPS (a temporary backup battery power unit). If the answer to either of these questions is No, quietly plug the thing in and flip the computer's power switch. (It's something *anybody* could overlook, but I wouldn't tell anyone if I were you.)

- **Are you sure that the monitor is on?** (Maybe it's just so quiet you don't hear it breathing.) Turn the monitor brightness dial all the way to the right. If the monitor's on, it should come blazing into life. If there's no power, it will sit there staring blankly at you. If your computer is humming and the power light is on, but you don't see anything on the screen, your monitor may be out. If you get no response, try plugging a different monitor into your system unit. Chances are, it's the monitor — not the computer system itself — that is the problem.

🔊**Are all the cables tight?** Turn the power switch to Off (on the PC, the monitor, and the power strip) and then make sure that everything is plugged in securely. Pull the cables out of the outlet strip and push them back in; do the same with the connection to the rear of the system unit. Do the cables one at a time so that they get plugged back into the right holes. Push everything in that can be pushed; tighten things with thumb-screws; get the miniscrewdriver for those nasty little connectors with screws (remember to turn that power off!). Then, after you're sure that everything is tight, turn the power back on. (And keep your fingers crossed.)

🔊**Is the computer locked?** Some people actually keep their systems under lock and key. The little silver lock on the front of the system may be turned to the Locked position (if the key's not in the lock, you may be in trouble). If the key is there, try turning it to the other position and attempt to restart your computer. If you don't have a key, skip this one.

🔊**Did you check the outlet?** Check to see whether other items are working in that particular outlet or surge protector strip. Maybe you blew a fuse (before you blew a gasket, that is).

If none of these things help, you may have something — *gulp* — more serious going on. Time for the witch doctor. (See sidebar "What Is a Witch Doctor?")

A Computer Hanging

Poison: A frozen computer

One day, you walk into the office, punch the power button on your computer, and it appears to blink into life without a hitch. You go get your cup of coffee, and you're ready to settle in for a long day's work.

But when you come back, you realize that your computer is playing statue. It apparently began its regular routine at startup (you heard all the familiar beeps and whirring sounds) but then froze in the middle of things.

Antidote: Your only recourse now may be to reboot (restart) your computer. (See Techie Term sidebar for *reboot.*)

If your computer hangs (that is, won't budge) again when you restart it, there may be a problem with one of the files your computer uses at startup (namely, CONFIG.SYS and AUTOEXEC.BAT). If this situation seems to be the problem, stick your

foot out the next time a technically savvy (witch doctor-looking) person walks by your desk and use the opportunity to get some free advice. If there are no witch doctors around and you're feeling bold, try the following suggeston.

Try restarting your computer with your system disk (providing you have one, of course — if you don't, see sidebar "How to Make a DOS System Disk"). If you get to an "A:\>" prompt, that's a good sign. It means the problem is somewhere in either CONFIG.SYS or AUTOEXEC.BAT. Now you just need to figure out precisely where the problem is. If you have DOS 6, you can tell DOS to either bypass CONFIG.SYS and AUTOEXEC.BAT entirely or step through them one line at a time (see Words of Wisdom sidebar).

First, look at the monitor. Immediately after you turn on your computer, a lot of otherwise meaningless text begins

Techie Term

Reboot means to restart your computer. You can do a *warm boot* of the computer one of two ways: by pressing and holding the Ctrl and Alt keys and then pressing Del, or by pressing the reset button on the front of your computer. If your system is really locked, it may not respond to these keystrokes. In that case, do a *cold boot* (a hardware boot) by turning the power off, *counting to ten* (put away that baseball bat), and turning the power back on.

scrolling across your screen. Get out your handy yellow office pad and begin writing. Don't worry if some things have alreay disappeared off the top of the screen — concentrate on what's still there, particularly the last thing your computer did. Is there an obvious DOS error message? Write it down. Look it up in the index of this book. Call the witch doctor. Scream, if you have to.

How to Make a DOS System Disk

All of the best witch doctors carry special medicines that they can pull out in an emergency. Here's a secret one that you can make yourself and carry in your satchel.

Just in case your computer hangs itself midsession, you need to have a System Disk already made and ready to be whipped into action. A DOS System Disk is just a disk that includes the DOS commands needed to start the computer. To add the system commands to the disk, type the following:

```
FORMAT A:/S
```

Once you're done creating it, find another floppy and use the DISKCOPY command to completely duplicate your System Disk. Store the disks nearby where you can find them. (I have a disk box for such things labeled "Safe Place." Don't laugh; it works!)

Now that you've got a mild-mannered DOS system disk, you're ready to turn it into a save-your-bacon System Survival Disk. See Chapter 2, "How to Make a DOS Startup Disk" for an alternative to the System Disk that can really save your life.

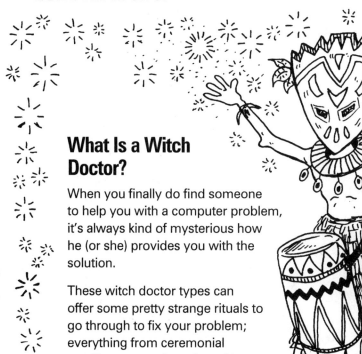

What Is a Witch Doctor?

When you finally do find someone to help you with a computer problem, it's always kind of mysterious how he (or she) provides you with the solution.

These witch doctor types can offer some pretty strange rituals to go through to fix your problem; everything from ceremonial sacrifices to magic potions. You can't live without them though. I mean, what else are you gonna do when your computer gets possessed?

So go ahead and eat that crunchy bug if they tell you to (even if it tastes bad) because you may have no other choice. Before you do though, make sure that you've found a true witch doctor (there are lots of quacks you know). To learn how to find a good one, see Chapter 2.

For additional advice about how to facilitate your interactions with witch doctors (and hopefully increase the chances of solving your problem), look for these witch doctor sidebars throughout the book.

Bringing Your Computer into the Present

Poison: "Today is *what?*"

Well, the computer started. It beeped and clunked and flashed a few things on the screen too quick for you to see them. And now it sits patiently, telling you that today is January 1, 1980.

The computer relies on the power of a small battery to keep track of the time and the date. When the battery runs out of juice (as they all do sooner or later), your computer is going to go into a flashback, stamping all your files with a prehistoric date and time.

Antidote: You can fix the problem temporarily — for this work session — by simply entering the right time and date at the prompts that appear when you start the system. Type **TIME** and press Enter. DOS displays the current time (as DOS sees it, anyway) and asks for the new time. Type the new time in the format hh:mm, like 12:05. Press Enter.

Enter the date the same way. Type **DATE** and press Enter. When DOS asks for it, type the correct date in the format mm-dd-yy, like 12-24-94. Press Enter.

If this doesn't work, it's time to build a sundial or one of those Stonehenge things. Over the long haul, however, you'll need to change the battery. (See "CMOS RAM error" later in this chapter.)

To solve this battery problem, you can open up the system unit yourself and look for the battery (it's back by the power supply in the back corner of your system). If you're sickened by the sight of exposed capacitors, however, it's best to let a PC surgeon fix it for you. A simple battery change takes a few seconds, no more (and usually costs less than $20).

Warning: Be sure to turn the system off *and* unplug it from the wall whenever you are poking around inside.

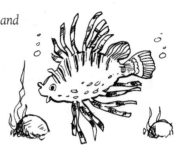

If you're using an older model PC — such as an XT or AT — you may need to run a program called Setup to reset the date and time so that they stick.

Here's Beeping at You, Kid

Poison: A beeping computer

Wow — this time the computer started, but you wish it wouldn't have. *Beep, beep, beep,* like a loud busy signal you can't turn off. What's wrong with the thing? You're not sure, but it sounds really mad.

Antidote: While you can still stand it, look at the screen. Is there a message there for you? (Ordinarily, you'll see some kind of error message with incessant beeping.) If so, jot down or memorize the error message so that you can look it up later. If there isn't a message, turn everything off. Quick.

The computer is probably not going to self-destruct, but it *is* trying to tell you something. Most likely, that something is that one of the important parts of your system — such as the keyboard — isn't connected properly.

Something may be lying on the keyboard (like this book) and holding down a key.

If the beeps have a distinct pattern (short-long-short, and so on), it's an error message; write down what you hear and call the witch doctor.

To cure incessant beeping, turn the power off, make sure that everything is plugged in securely, and turn the power back on. (Or get ear plugs.)

When Your Computer Fails Its Own Test

Through wind, rain, snow, biting dogs, and dustballs (well, maybe not rain and snow), our computers are expected to function. You need them to work the way they are supposed to.

One way the computer makes sure that it is performing up to snuff is through the use of a POST, or Power-On-Self-Test. When you flip the power switch on, the computer goes through a series of tests to make sure that everything is in working order. If something is on the blink, your computer either locks up, displays some sort of cryptic secret message on your screen, or beeps in a distinct pattern.

Poison: A computer that fails the POST

If you can, follow the instructions you see. Doing this isn't going to make the problem go away, but it may give you time to copy any valuable files before your PC completely seizes up. If following the instructions doesn't get you any further, try doing a soft boot (Ctrl-Alt-Delete). If your computer starts this time, *immediately* back up anything you care about, and then call the witch doctor. If it continues to play ignorant, cross your fingers and start beating out "come hither, Witch Doctor" on the ceremonial drum.

How can a computer fail a test when it knows all of the answers? Go figure.

Well, if you really must know, the POST test checks your computer's video board, keyboard, and memory. POST errors usually occur when you've changed something involving your hardware, such as changing the configuration or adding or removing expansion boards. If you're really ob-

sessed with this POST thing and want to know more, read *PC SECRETS* (1992, IDG), or *Upgrading and Fixing PCs For Dummies* (1993, IDG).

Three Oh-No! Errors During Setup

It's likely that Santa brought your computer to you with DOS already installed. Literally all PCs have some sort of DOS from the time they leave the sales floor. If you purchased your system piece by piece through mail-order catalogs, you may have to install DOS yourself. If so, see *DOS For Dummies* (1993, IDG).

Warning: Before you upgrade, make a backup of your system, especially if you're going to install DoubleSpace (DOS's new compression utility).

Poison: Error messages during installation

Antidote: Just in case things don't go well when you try to install DOS, here are a few On-No! error messages to look out for:

There is not enough free space on drive C to install MS-DOS

This isn't a good sign. It's not fatal, however. You'll need to back out of the Setup program (by pressing F3) and delete or compress some of the files on your hard disk to make more room.

Cannot find a hard disk on your computer

For some reason, DOS is not seeing the hard disk. Are you sure that you have one? (Sorry, I had to ask.) If you have one, are you sure that it's working properly? Unless you have a really odd model of hard drive that is not supported by DOS, something squirrelly is going on with your hard drive. Back out of Setup and run a diagnostics program such as Norton Disk Doctor (see Techie Term sidebar). Chances are, it's time to call your local witch doctor.

Incompatible hard disk or device driver

This is a shade better than the last one. At least DOS is seeing the drive, but DOS doesn't recognize what it sees. If you have a specialized partition on your hard drive,

Techie Term

A *diagnostic program* is one that looks over your disk or hard disk and finds out what the trouble is. Some examples are PC Tools, Norton Utilities, and MSD (the Microsoft diagnostics tool that comes with later versions of DOS).

a removable hard disk, or a Bernoulli drive, you may need some extra tips for setting up DOS 6.2. Check your manual to see whether your setup qualifies for assistance or give those tech support aficionados a call.

Words of Wisdom: Bypassing

DOS 6.2 now allows you to *bypass* or step through commands in your AUTOEXEC.BAT and other batch programs. (MS-DOS 6 only enabled you to do this with your CONFIG.SYS file.) Witch doctors know that this is an invaluable feature when trying to troubleshoot problems during startup. It's similar to using REM to help isolate a problem. (See Chapter 2 for a discussion of REM.)

While you see the message Starting MS-DOS..., you can do the following:

- Press the F5 key to bypass all of the commands in the AUTOEXEC.BAT and CONFIG.SYS files.

- Press the F8 key to bypass individual commands in the AUTOEXEC.BAT and CONFIG.SYS files.

- Press Ctrl-F5 to bypass DoubleSpace and to bypass all of the commands in the AUTOEXEC.BAT and CONFIG.SYS files.

- Press Ctrl-F8 to bypass DoubleSpace and to bypass individual commands in the AUTOEXEC.BAT and CONFIG.SYS files.

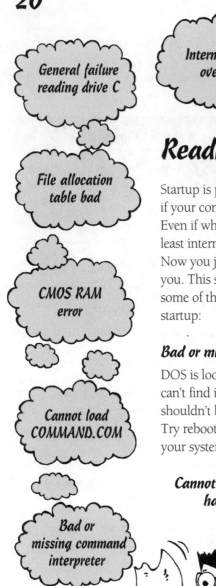

General failure reading drive C

Internal stack overflow

Invalid date

File allocation table bad

CMOS RAM error

Cannot load COMMAND.COM

Bad or missing command interpreter

Reading Smoke Signals

Startup is pretty scary, huh? Remember that if your computer comes on, it's a good sign. Even if what you see is an error message, at least internally your computer is functioning. Now you just have to decipher what it's telling you. This section lists, in alphabetic order, some of the error messages you may see at startup:

Bad or missing command interpreter

DOS is looking for COMMAND.COM and can't find it. Is there a disk in drive A that shouldn't be there (such as a bad boot disk)? Try rebooting, and, if that doesn't work, use your system disk.

Cannot load COMMAND.COM, system halted

Oooh, not a good sign. Something bad has happened to your COMMAND.COM file. Still have your DOS system disk? Good. Start your computer with that disk and then copy

COMMAND.COM over to the hard disk by typing the command line

```
COPY A:COMMAND.COM C:\
```

and pressing Enter. Then reboot.

CMOS RAM error

Remember the battery that takes care of the time and date? It powers CMOS (yes, it's pronounced *sea-moss*), a special memory chip that also stores some important settings that your computer uses. The battery backs up the CMOS setup information. If the battery "goes," the system may think it has no disk drives (a problem). Witch doctor time again. Have a techie take a look.

File allocation table bad

Believe me, you don't want to see this error. (But it's probably nothing *you* did wrong.) Turn your computer off and go to lunch. A good, long lunch. When you feel able to face your afternoon, you'll need to get help. This isn't something you can face alone.

A file allocation table, or FAT (see Chapter 3), is like an index that DOS uses to remember which files go where. Both hard disks and floppy disks have file allocation tables. When a table goes bad, DOS doesn't know how to find the files it needs. Only a person with substantial DOS experience (and a high threshhold for pain) should attempt to fix this kind of error.

General failure reading drive C

Sorry to hit you with two Bad News items in a row, but this is another poison dart you can live without. This error message is telling you that DOS can't read the information on your hard drive. Ouch. If the error message is General failure reading drive A, it's not quite as serious, although it most likely means your disk drive needs to have its reading glasses readjusted.

You may be able to get around the General failure error — even on drive C — by using your DOS System Disk. Put the disk in the drive and reboot, and then change over to drive C by typing **C:** and pressing Enter. You may be able to solve the problem temporarily by using a utility such as Norton Disk Doctor. But it is a good idea to seek help from your local witch doctor anyway.

Internal stack overflow. System halted

Even computers, with their capability of processing information at the speed of light, must do things one at a time. A stack overflow error occurs when too much is happening too fast and your computer can't deal with all the interaction at once. Each time one portion of your system requests an action from the microprocessor, that request gets placed on a stack. A stack overflow occurs when too many demands are made in too short a period. Chances are, if you write down the error and entice the nearest witch doctor over to sleuth things out, the stack issue can be resolved with a simple modification to your CONFIG.SYS file. Let someone qualified do the surgery, however.

Invalid date

Depending on how your system is set up, you may or may not be responsible for setting your own date. If your computer comes up and gives you one of these

```
Enter new date (mm-dd-yy):
```

look at that line carefully. That's month month, day day, year year. With hyphens in between. In other words, if you type **09-24-93**, you're cool. If you type **September 24, 1993** or **09>24>93**, DOS is going to give you an Invalid date message. Use only dashes, hyphens, or periods to separate dates. If you give DOS what it wants, things go a lot better for you in the long run.

Keyboard error, press F2 to continue

Remember that incessant beeping problem? Keyboard connections are often the culprit. It's pretty safe to assume that even if you press F2, nothing is going to happen. (DOS isn't seeing your keyboard, right? Then how will it know that you have pressed F2?) Plug in all the cables — or just give them an extra push to make sure that they're tight — and reboot your computer. If the beeping stops, cool. If it doesn't, start looking for a keyboard technician.

Also, try the following: Remove the keyboard plug, hold it close to your mouth, and breathe on it. That puts some moisture on the contacts and often solves the problem. Of course, you still need to plug it back in. This tip works on *any* cable contact-related problem.

Non-system disk or disk error. Replace and press any key when ready.

This is perhaps the most common of all initial startup messages and the easiest to solve. (In fact — don't tell — I got that error this morning.) This is one of those darn-it messages that occur when you've forgotten to do something, such as open the door on drive A when you've got a nonbootable disk in the drive. The solution? Just open the drive door (or take out the disk on 3.5" drives) and press Enter.

For later versions of DOS, if you've recently completed a backup (good for you!) but left the last backup disk in the drive (bye-bye brownie points), you'll see

```
Non-system disk or disk error
Microsoft backup diskette
```

when you boot. Be sure to remove the disk and put it with its brethren.

You Know You're Really in Trouble When . . .

Something starts smoking

Does this ever really happen? Logic tells us No. Friends who perversely
enjoy trading computer war stories and making us quake in our boots say
Yes. You may not see the smoke, but it is possible to smell that electrical
odor that tells you that something inside is going very, very wrong. Turn
the computer off immediately (and the monitor and the surge protector,
too) and call someone who's immune to electrical shocks. (Whatever you
do, don't throw water on it.)

When you can't find a witch doctor

If there are no witch doctors to be found, try finding the answers yourself by checking out the following places:

- The help system in your software
- The manuals that come with the software
- BBS on-line help
- Third-party books from the library or bookstore

The fan sounds like an airplane motor

This doesn't always mean you're headed for the big cooling fan in the sky, but it should definitely be taken as a warning signal. Report any unnatural occurrences to the appropriate governing bodies immediately.

You hear an electrical ZAP! and the monitor flashes out

Oh, you can try rebooting, but you know in your heart that it's useless. That monitor's history. How often does this stuff happen? Sometime between rarely and never. (But don't you appreciate the happy, gleaming face of your monitor more now?)

You get no signs of life no matter what you do

Well, DOS isn't going to help you out of this one. DOS is inside the system unit, kicked back, feet propped up, saying "Well, guys, see you in a few days. You don't expect me to work under *these* conditions, do you?" Time to call the witch doctor to get that lazy program back to work.

Chapter 2   DOS Doesn't Like Me

Paths through Peril

Well, look at it this way. You survived the first leg of the journey, which means that your computer is, at least, functioning. You've loaded DOS successfully (or so it seems). Now you're ready to take on those pesky problems that occur in the first tender hours of DOS life.

It was a dark and stormy night . . . that first night on DOS island, that is. And from then on, it seems like the whole world is against you.

The Long, Hot CPU

On the dune side of the island, it's hot. Very hot. Things are pretty steamy these days, thanks to a high-pressure cell pushing in the dry desert heat. Having something go wrong with your CPU can really make blood pressure boil — especially if you're the one trying to fix the problem. If I were you, I wouldn't tell the tech support person you caused the following problems:

- The thing doesn't turn on since you knocked your Coke over on the desktop.

- You decided to run some memory-management program a stranger in an overcoat handed you.

🔷 You unplugged everything in back so you could move your computer and now you can't figure out what goes where.

🔷 You put those cute little slogan refrigerator magnets all over the side of your system unit, and now things are really going bonkers.

🔷 You tried to use your computer as a tower system (even though it's a desktop system), and you accidentally kicked it over.

🔷 You didn't realize that you were supposed to turn the little thumb-screws on the cable, and so you just pulled with all your might. Now the printer won't work.

How to Make a DOS Startup Disk

Sometimes a *system disk* (see Chapter 1 sidebar about FORMAT /S) is not enough to get you going again. You need the more robust *startup disk* to start your computer when you're having problems. (If you have neither a system disk or a startup disk, try using the Setup Disk 1 for DOS or your Uninstall disk that you created when you installed DOS.)

To create a startup disk, insert the DOS Setup Disk 1 in drive B (or A, if it's not compatible). Type

`a:/setup /f`   **or**   `b:/setup /f`

and follow the instructions. When the process is complete, you will have the system files that you need and many useful commands on your startup disk. You can use the COPY command to add these files manually to your system disk also. You'll find these in your DOS subdirectory — I've written the names with wildcards because the extensions sometimes vary between DOS versions:

- CHKDSK.*	- MSD.*	*New with DOS 6*
- EDIT.*	- QBASIC.*	- SCANDISK.*
- FDISK.*	- UNDELETE.*	- MSAV.*
- FORMAT.*	- UNFORMAT.*	- VSAFE.*
- MEM.*	- XCOPY.*	- MSBACKUP.*

Unrecognized Commands at Startup

Poison: One of the following messages Unrecognized command in CONFIG.SYS or AUTOEXEC.BAT. Error in line x. or Bad command or file name flashes briefly on your screen during startup.

This error is sometimes elusive because the computer may never really stop to tell you about it. When DOS is busy getting your computer started, it tends to just blow right through problems in the CONFIG.SYS and AUTOEXEC.BAT files without saying much of anything. In fact, you may not know something is wrong until a program fails for no apparent reason and the Twilight Zone theme music fades in around you. . . .

Antidote: Reboot and watch the screen carefully.

With DOS 6:

If you've got DOS 6, troubleshooting this error is a breeze.

Reboot your computer, and then press the F8 key briefly when the screen says Starting MS-DOS. . . . F8 is an interruption key (F5, Ctrl-F5, and Ctrl-F8 are the others — see Chapter 1 for information). It "interrupts" the normal startup process and makes DOS ask you for permission before running each command in the CONFIG.SYS and AUTOEXEC.BAT files. Finding the problem from there is pretty easy. Each command executes before the system asks you about the next one. When DOS tries one that isn't working, you'll see the error message immediately, along with the command line in question. Poof! There's your apparent culprit. Continue your troubleshooting from there (cross-reference the specific error message in the index for more help).

With earlier versions of DOS:

Solving this the old-fashioned way takes some work, but you feel just as satisfied when you're done.

🐦 Start by making backup copies of your
AUTOEXEC.BAT and CONFIG.SYS files. See
the satchel in this section for details.

🐦 Determine which file needs attention. This is
relatively easy because the errors springing
from CONFIG.SYS conveniently say `Unrecog-`
`nized command in CONFIG.SYS` and then give
you the exact line number DOS didn't like. If your error is `Bad com-`
`mand or file name`, you'll be working with AUTOEXEC.BAT. If it is
something other than these two, you probably should see call your
witch doctor.

🐦 From the root directory, open the appropriate file for editing. Make
sure you're in the root directory of drive C:. The specific command is
either **EDIT AUTOEXEC.BAT** or **EDIT CONFIG.SYS**, depending on your
selection in the previous step. If you've been living right, DOS's EDIT
program will start and your file will automatically load.

🐦 For CONFIG.SYS problems, look at the line number DOS complained
about in the original error message (you *did* write that down, didn't
you? If not, exit the editor and reboot the computer, paying closer
attention to the error this time). Do you recognize the command at all?
(If not, call the witch doctor for help before trying anything else.) Is the
command spelled right? Does the line mention some device you no
longer have (such as a specific printer, CD-ROM drive, or external tape
backup)? Try putting REM at the beginning of the line in question. Exit
the editor (press Alt-F, X, and then Y to save changes) and reboot.

🐦 Does the error happen again? If not, it looks like you've found the
problem. Try doing some "normal" things, such as running your word
processor or spreadsheet program. If you don't notice anything acting
strangely, the line in question may have just outlived its time. But if
one of your programs is acting weird, call the witch doctor and tell him
what you've done so far.

🐦 Did *more* errors come up this time? This is *definitely* witch doctor time.
The command you've REMmed out apparently supports other commands, which are now collectively distressed. Don't worry, though —
you didn't hurt anything. Fill the witch doctor in on your troubleshooting steps to this point and let him take over.

➥ For AUTOEXEC.BAT errors, start with the **second** command in the file and type **REM** at the beginning of each line (see Words of Wisdom in this chapter for more information). By REMming out everything except line 1, you've established a place to start testing.

➥ Exit the editor (press Alt-F, X, and then Y to save changes) and restart your computer. If the error doesn't come up this time, go back to the last step and remove the REM from the next command. Save your file, exit the editor, and reboot. Keep doing this until the error comes back. (If it *never* comes back, shrug your shoulders and go on with life, but make a mental note of the symptom you noticed; if it keeps happening, call in the witch doctor.)

➥ Once the error recurs, you've potentially identified the culprit. Either continue troubleshooting on your own or proudly call your witch doctor with the news that you've worked through the problem this far and would like some assistance to finish the job.

Screen Blips and Other Annoyances

Poison: Your screen seems to shimmy or waver. It jiggles, wiggles, wobbles, and otherwise imitates jello. And it's slowly driving you nuts.

This isn't a DOS thing. It isn't even a software thing. But it can still cause quite a few headaches and rack up a nice little pile of computer repair bills.

Antidote: I hate to tell you, but this could be a "feature" of your monitor. There are some other options, too; so don't get depressed this early in the process. Save it up and get *seriously* depressed later.

➥ **Is it interlaced?** If the screen seems to almost imperceptibly jump, particularly in Windows or other graphically based software, you may have an interlaced monitor. If so, that's just its nature. When the monitor updates (*refreshes*) its screen, it either redraws the lines one right after another (noninterlaced), or it draws all the odd ones first and then goes back and does the even ones (interlaced). The jiggle you perceive is the *interlacing* — you're seeing the slight differences between the even and odd lines. Sad to say, but the only "fix" is to spring for a new monitor. Noninterlaced monitors cost more than interlaced monitors, but the difference is worth it.

Have you checked the control knobs? Does the screen waver? Is it off to one side? Is there an annoying line that moves through it (like when someone has messed with the horizontal-hold control on the old Zenith)? Somewhere on your monitor, you should have some control knobs for adjusting the display. Fiddle with these controls and see if it helps.

Is it just the colors? Choose a different color scheme in your application. If you choose a color scheme that enhances the contrast between the background colors and the displayed text, it may ease the strain on your eyes and, hopefully, improve the overall look.

Is it interference? If your screen has a slow wave in it, you may have an electrical interference problem. Is your monitor sitting on or next to something, like your laser printer or combination micro-wave-stereo-toaster oven with 14-day advance program-ming?

Turn off anything electrical near the monitor. Does the problem go
away?

Is it broken? If possible, try your monitor with another computer,
physically away from your normal work area. If the problem persists
there, you know it's the monitor. (Some monitors wobble so obviously
that you know there's something wrong. If yours is one of those, have
it serviced before things get worse.) If the problem goes away, there's
something screwy about your workspace. Get a witch doctor to help.
Ask him to check out your graphics card and your video drivers. And
tell him to see what's behind that wall near your computer. It could be
an enormous magnet or a nuclear power plant or something.

DOS Prompt Problems and Preferences

Poison: A dull, uninformative prompt

We could fill an entire book with complaints about the DOS prompt. It's
rude. It's unfriendly. Not sympathetic at all. No humor, no spark. You can
make your otherwise uncooperative prompt friendlier by using the
PROMPT command.

Think about it. You walk into work in the morning, flip your computer
into life, and see C>. Not very polite. If you want your prompt to tell you
what the current directory is and how you got there, type the following:

```
PROMPT $P$G
```

Now you get the world's most popular prompt (C:\>). There are lots of
other variations, but seeking out the dark secrets of PROMPTing is reserved
for people with too much time on their hands. If you simply must know
more, type **HELP PROMPT** for the sordid details.

To make your new prompt permanent, add the PROMPT command (as in
PROMPT PG) to your AUTOEXEC.BAT file. If there's a PROMPT command there already, change it to your liking.

For help with editing the AUTOEXEC.BAT and CONFIG.SYS files, see
DOS For Dummies. If this doesn't help, see the next edition of *Lifestyles of
the Lost and Starving*.

Note: So, 257 million PROMPT PG commands later, the DOS
programmers *finally* sat up and took notice. In DOS 6.x, the prompt
is C:\> by default, not C>. The decade-long PROMPT debacle is
hereby ended. Hooray, programmers!

Bad Command or File Name

The most common problem happens after you type a
command (or what you *thought* was a command),
press Enter, and DOS sends up a smoke signal.
(Hey, that command worked a minute ago.)

First, the tidal wave . . .

Hmmm. You could be a victim of the commonest of all DOS faux pas — misplaced fingers. You meant to type **COPY**, your fingers thought they typed **COPY**, but DOS saw **CPOY**. What to do?

Type the command again, carefully this time, and press Enter. Double-check what you just typed by pressing F3 before you type anything else. F3 redisplays the most recently entered command at the DOS prompt. (See Chapter 7 for more about DOS commands.)

When you retype the command, make sure you consider the following DOS conventions:

➧ **Careful with the spaces**. DOS will put up with spaces between words or parts of a command (like when you type COPY A:FILENAME C:), but it won't put up with spaces in file names. It may also get grumpy with you if you put too many spaces in one place. One will do, thank you very much. Instead of Bad command or file name, you may see Syntax error (particularly in older versions of DOS). Same thing.

➧ **Get the right name**. The challenging part of naming your files is providing enough informa-tion in the name so that you'll recognize it again later. But DOS only gives you eight letters in which to do that. Remember, when you're entering a file name (either at the DOS prompt or somewhere else) that entering a name of more than eight characters (not counting the three-

Prompt Etiquette
Some people go really hog-wild with their prompts. Others fall victim to those people who think it's funny to change your prompt while you're away from your desk. One particularly obnoxious computer prankster changed a neophyte's prompt to the following:

```
C:\> Format Drive C:
Press any key to continue...>
```

Not a real nice thing to do.

character extension after the period) will display an error. For more information on working with files (and that means file names, too), see Chapter 4.

🖐 **Watch that symbolism.** DOS is also finicky about how you use punctuation symbols in your command lines. The asterisk (*), question mark (?), backslash (/), and forward slash (\) all have particular uses. (See *DOS For Dummies* for more about wildcards.) Mixing up the two slashes is a very common problem. The backslash (/) is the "parameter" slash. Use it to give DOS commands more information (like telling DIR to stop after each page by typing **DIR/P**). The forward slash (\) is the "subdirectory" slash. It goes in path names *only* (as in C:\FORWARD.HRE).

🖐 **Not all commands have nicknames.** Although it's possible to shorten some DOS commands (DEL for DELETE, REN for RENAME, and so on), not all DOS commands can be shortened to a three-letter abbreviation. FORMAT can't be FOR, and DISKCOPY can't be DIS.

If you entered a command and got the Bad command or file name error — and you're sure that you entered it correctly — consider whether you're in the right directory. If you tried to start a program from the wrong directory, you'll get this error.

For directory assistance, dial Chapter 5.

Getting Rid of an Unwanted Shell

Poison: Unwanted DOS shell loads automatically

Here's a different problem: You've got a DOS shell that is rigged to come up automatically, and you're just sick of dealing with its loud face first thing in the morning. You are not a morning person and would rather have a DOS prompt that's more your speed: quiet. Nothing exciting. Not much to look at. Well, someone has thoughtfully done you a favor by putting the DOSSHELL command in your

AUTOEXEC.BAT file so the thing would load automatically when your system booted.

Antidote: You can remove the annoyance by deleting the line from AUTOEXEC.BAT (or by typing REM at the beginning of the line to make it a comment line). (Type **EDIT** at the C> prompt and open AUTOEXEC.BAT. But be sure to save a copy of the file before you edit it.)

Then the hurricane . . .

How to Make a Backup Copy of AUTOEXEC.BAT and CONFIG.SYS

Before you make changes to these important files, always make a backup. Put a blank, formatted disk in drive A and, from the root directory of drive C (your prompt should show C:\), type

```
COPY AUTOEXEC.BAT A:
```

and

```
COPY CONFIG.SYS A:
```

and press Enter after each line. Label the disk and put it in a safe place.

To make a copy on your hard drive, do the following procedure. From the root directory (your prompt should say C:\>), type

```
COPY AUTOEXEC.BAT AUTOEXEC.XXX
```

I usually name the copies AUTOEXEC.XXX and CONFIG.XXX, but feel free to come up with something more clever. Repeat the process for CONFIG.SYS.

When you're done, print out a copy of the files as well. The next time you talk to a witch doctor, make an offering to him of these backup files and printouts. He will appreciate it.

Where to Go to Find a Good Witch Doctor

Even though they're not behind every palm tree, you'll find witch doctors all over the place:

➡ The technical support staff (the "help desk" or IS department) of your corporation

➡ The staff who provide technical support by phone for the software and hardware manufacturers of your program or system (there may be a fee)

➡ Trainers at computer training centers (some provide support after you take their classes)

➡ The experienced coworker in the next cubicle

➡ The increasingly popular private consultants

➡ Knowledgeable staff at computer retail/service stores

➡ Members of your local computer society or user groups

➡ Your friends, your parents, your neighbors, your kids!

The Case of the Invisible or Misbehaving Mouse

Poison: Mouse won't work with the DOS shell or a DOS application

It's really swell that the newest application software gives you menus and buttons and other things to make your life easier, but that doesn't help much when your mouse goes belly-button-up.

Antidote: Mouse problems are pretty easy to solve. In general terms, the problem is in the mouse itself, in its connection to the computer, or in the software. (And by the way, before you try the following steps, make sure that your application actually does support a mouse.)

➡ **Do you have a mouse driver loaded?** (Driver? Huh? — see Techie Term sidebar.) The most common drivers are MOUSE.SYS and MOUSE.COM. They come with most versions of DOS prior to version 6. If you have a non-Microsoft mouse, you probably have a custom driver written especially for it. See your mouse's documentation for details. DOS 6.2 includes *only* MOUSE.COM. During installation, DOS 6.2 searches both the CONFIG.SYS and AUTOEXEC.BAT files for any reference to a mouse driver. It

Techie Term

A *device driver* (often shortened to just *driver*) is software that explains how DOS should interact with a particular device, such as a mouse, a printer, or a CD-ROM drive. DOS, being basically brain-dead, requires alot of help in this area. If you cruise through your CONFIG.SYS and AUTOEXEC.BAT files, you'll likely see references to drivers with names like MOUSE.COM and MSCDEX.EXE.

REM's out whatever it finds and inserts its own MOUSE command into AUTOEXEC.BAT. Isn't that nice?

🖱 **Does DOS say that it finds your mouse?** When you boot, watch for the mouse driver to load. Most mouse drivers check for the mouse before they load. The standard Microsoft driver that comes with DOS tells you on-screen whether or not it found your mouse. If the driver loads without a hitch, you know your mouse is connected. If the driver can't find the mouse, go on to the following step. (**Note:** Some mouse drivers come with test routines you can use to make sure that the mouse is behaving correctly.)

🖱 **Does the mouse work with other DOS programs?** If so, make sure your application software is configured correctly. Do you have to *tell* it about your mouse or does it automatically look to see if you have one? Do you have to explain specifically what mouse brand you own? You'd be amazed at how you have to spoon-feed some programs these days. If your application is an electronic toddler, sit down with it and explain all about the birds, the bees, and the mouses.

Is it plugged into the right port? Is it plugged in at all? Check the mouse's connection to the computer. Some computers have a dedicated mouse port (usually with a small, round connector called a mini-DIN or PS/2 mouse connector). You might also have a standard serial mouse with either a 9- or 25-pin plug on it. Regardless of the specifics, make sure it's plugged in tightly. If it is, and you're still having trouble, it could be bleak. Some well-meaning folks may even tell you to prepare to hold a really big wake and start hoping for that $59 mouse special.

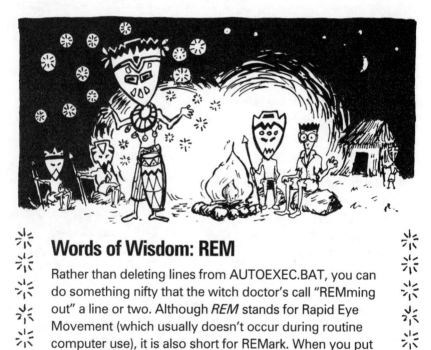

Words of Wisdom: REM

Rather than deleting lines from AUTOEXEC.BAT, you can do something nifty that the witch doctor's call "REMming out" a line or two. Although *REM* stands for Rapid Eye Movement (which usually doesn't occur during routine computer use), it is also short for REMark. When you put the word REM in front of a line in AUTOEXEC.BAT, it turns the line into a remark, which means that DOS will just read the line and say "Oh, that's interesting," but it won't execute the instruction included in the line. Once you check out the problem, you can return the line to normal by deleting the REM. (Later versions of DOS let you use a semicolon rather than using REM.)

➡ **Did you try rebooting?** But stop and think for a minute. You're forgetting one of the most basic rules of troubleshooting PCs: Before you do anything else, try again. Start fresh. Do exactly the same thing one more time. Shouldn't make any difference, right? Wrong. Sometimes these machines get cranky and just won't wake up the first time. Mice are no different. Try turning everything off (or at least resetting it), and turn it all on again. This technique often works with most computer-related devices, including modems and printers. Does your mouse work now? It does? But why? Who cares. As long as it works now, just count your PC blessings.

If nothing gets your mouse's attention, you may have a dead rodent. Call your witch doctor and tell him that Whitey bit the dust.

And the floods — they're horrendous. It just isn't fair. What else can possibly go wrong?

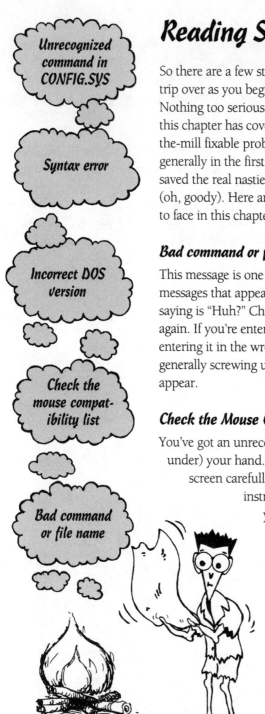

Reading Smoke Signals

So there are a few stumbling blocks you may trip over as you begin your DOS experience. Nothing too serious, though. That's because this chapter has covered some of your run-of-the-mill fixable problems that crop up generally in the first few days of DOS use. I've saved the real nasties for the chapters to come (oh, goody). Here are the only errors you have to face in this chapter:

Bad command or file name

This message is one of those catch-all error messages that appear when what DOS is really saying is "Huh?" Check your typing and try again. If you're entering the wrong thing, entering it in the wrong directory, or just generally screwing up, this message will appear.

Check the Mouse Compatibility List

You've got an unrecognizable mouse on (or under) your hand. Read the message on the screen carefully and look up your mouse instructions. For some mice, you may need to contact the manufacturer to get an updated mouse driver. (See the section earlier in the chapter under "The Case of the Invisible or Misbehaving Mouse.")

Incorrect DOS version

Well, you know that it's supposed to work.
Your DOS manual (gasp — you really
looked?) tells you so. You type a
command and DOS shrugs its
shoulders.

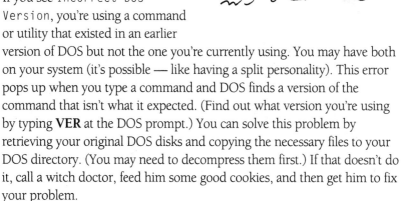

If you see Incorrect DOS
Version, you're using a command
or utility that existed in an earlier
version of DOS but not the one you're currently using. You may have both
on your system (it's possible — like having a split personality). This error
pops up when you type a command and DOS finds a version of the
command that isn't what it expected. (Find out what version you're using
by typing **VER** at the DOS prompt.) You can solve this problem by
retrieving your original DOS disks and copying the necessary files to your
DOS directory. (You may need to decompress them first.) If that doesn't do
it, call a witch doctor, feed him some good cookies, and then get him to fix
your problem.

Syntax error

Here's another one that is a general, you-didn't-type-this-right kind of
error. Check your spelling and the spacing in the command line and press
Enter. You may see this message in older versions of DOS.

Unrecognized command in CONFIG.SYS

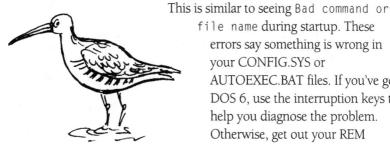

This is similar to seeing Bad command or
file name during startup. These
errors say something is wrong in
your CONFIG.SYS or
AUTOEXEC.BAT files. If you've got
DOS 6, use the interruption keys to
help you diagnose the problem.
Otherwise, get out your REM
command and go sleuthing.

You Know You're Really in Trouble When . . .

You get an Error in EXE file message

This message is another biggie that doesn't have anything to do with DOS — usually. It shows up when DOS is trying to load the program you selected and something isn't working the way it should.

Sometimes the culprit is a DOS EXE file (DOS has a number of EXE files — do a DIR *.EXE of your DOS directory). But often, the problem is related to an EXE file belonging to the program you're trying to load.

In any case, try copying the

faulty EXE file from the original disks. If you still get the error, contact the program's manufacturer.

You see the Divide overflow message

This error message is a really unfriendly one that makes no sense. Divide overflow? Something was divided (perhaps unequally), and one part of it is flowing over something it shouldn't?

Don't try to figure it out. Some things in life are better left to programmers.

If you see this message, you were using a program that was on a fast track to nowhere. The program tried to perform a calculation that flopped, and you were left with a crashing program.

The problem isn't caused by DOS, so it's not something you did (or something you can fix). Just reboot your computer and try the program again. If you keep getting the same error message, contact the program's manufacturer.

Chapter 3

Disk Difficulties

Paths through Peril

Congratulations. You're still with us. Trudging right along, aren't you? Grab a vine and let's go. Now we're picking up the pace a bit by facing some of the annoyances you may run up against as you begin using DOS. One of the first things you'll do as a new DOS user is work with disks. So, hang on tight and here we go.

Obviously, this isn't such a friendly place after all. You aren't gonna let it get you down though. It's kind of a pretty place, actually . . . if you could just master this vine thing.

No matter what the perils, you know you'll succeed eventually. Besides, practice makes perfect, right? How bad can it be? But what do all of these scrolls mean?

Disk Dysfunction

There's only so much you can do to a disk. When they're sick, they're sick. When they're dead, they're dead.

The average floppy is going to give out sooner or later (usually later rather than sooner, if you are following proper care-and-feeding techniques).

Having a hard drive going bad is another matter. Usually a hard drive doesn't just die right in the middle of something. Like the rest of us, the hard drive shows symptoms of things going wrong before it totally goes south.

Here are some things to watch for:

- Strange errors that occur once or twice and then disappear
- A hard drive access light that stays on when it shouldn't
- Programs that take longer than usual to load and run
- Sudden errors that shut you down during a program

Just to be on the safe side, have someone well trained in internal medicine take a look at your system unit once every six months or so (or longer if your computer doesn't get much use).

Protecting Your Data

Poison: Floppy disks with **original** data on them

Antidote: Keep your originals on the hard drive and your backups on floppies.

Floppy disks *cannot* be trusted. They die if you look at them wrong. Never trust valuable *original* data to a floppy disk. Never, Never, Never, Never!!!

Never, that is, except if you're working on very sensitive files. From a security point of view, floppies are a great idea because they can be put away out of sight, safe from prying eyes. To make it a good idea from a computer standpoint, keep *at least* one (preferably two) backups of each diskette. Also, spend some extra money to get very high quality disks.

The Do-Nothing Disk: Sit and Spin

Poison: Do-nothing diskettes

Okay. DOS started, everything seems to work, and you're ready to get going. You put a disk in the drive. You enter the WHATEVER command. The little red light flashes on, and you hear a whirring sound emanating from the drive.

The whirring sound whirs and whirs.

And whirs.

And nothing else happens. Ever.

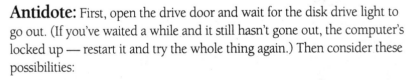

Antidote: First, open the drive door and wait for the disk drive light to go out. (If you've waited a while and it still hasn't gone out, the computer's locked up — restart it and try the whole thing again.) Then consider these possibilities:

- **Did you have the disk in right?** With the label up, toward you (both 5.25 and 3.5). If you're using a 5.25-inch disk, the two cute little notches go in first. If you're using a 3.5-inch disk, the shutter end (that's the metal piece) goes in first.

- **Did you close the drive door?** Many 5.25-inch drives have latches you need to close manually; the 3.5-inch doesn't have a door (so what did you close?). The 3.5-inch disk just pops into place when you push it in the drive slot.

Is there anything jamming the drive? Get out the trusty penlight flashlight and look up in there. No labels? No chewing gum? None of Aunt Edna's leftover fruit surprise?

After checking for improper placement and foreign substances, try again. Put the disk back in and reenter the command. Still whirring? Chances are, if you let it whir a while, it will eventually grind to a halt and display

```
General failure reading drive B
Abort, Retry, Fail?
```

Call for help.

Where Have You Been Lately?

Poison: I saved a backup copy of my document to a floppy. Now every time I do something the floppy light comes on; the commands take forever!

Antidote: Some programs (particularly in Windows)

keep track of which drive you've referred to lately. They assume (because they're insecure?) that since you're doing something out there, *they* should do something out there. Here's your simple fix:

1. Save your document to your hard drive again.

2. Remove the floppy disk.

Things should speed up significantly.

ARF! (Abort, Retry, Fail)

Poison: Dealing with ARF errors

The ARF message will appear when you do any of the following things:

➥ You try to use an unformatted disk

➥ You try to use an incompatible disk (like a Macintosh disk)

➥ You try to use a damaged disk

➥ You try to use a high-density disk in a low-density drive

Note: Instead of the ARF message, you may get ARI (Abort, Retry, Ignore).

Antidote: So what do you do about it? If you're sure the disk is formatted with the right operating system and you think DOS is just being fussy, pull the disk out and put it back in and try your command again. The disk just may not have been *seated* well in the drive. If you get the error again, press C (Cancel) or I (Ignore).

Warning: Pressing I for Ignore doesn't solve the problem; it merely tells DOS to blow it off right now.

At the DOS prompt, copy anything you care about from the failing disk to either your hard drive or another floppy *immediately*:

Use the COPY command (not XCOPY) to temporarily back up up the files.

You'll likely get another ARF/ARI message while you're doing this. It's OK; we knew it was coming.

ARI — Note which file DOS is trying to copy; then say "Ignore." Depending on how severe the error is, you may have to "Ignore" two or three times. COPY will blissfully continue pulling files from the disk. When it's done, use your list to erase the damaged file or files from your backup.

ARF — Retry a couple of times (that may not get you anywhere) and note the name of the file containing the error. Press "Cancel" and then use DIR to look at the directory. Manually copy files that come after the damaged file in the listing.

If the damaged file is *very* important, take the disk in question to your witch doctor. Sometimes she can retrieve at least something so it won't be a total loss.

Of course, if you already have a backup, you can toss your head back and laugh hysterically because you've beaten the machine at its own game.

Techie Term

Disks and disk drives come in two flavors: *high-density* and *double-density* (DD, although some people say "low" density). HD disks, used with a high-density drive, store information in a condensed format. They put two to four times more data into the same physical space than a DD disk can. High-density drives can use DD disks, but the disks don't magically turn into HD-capacity wonders; they're still just DD disks. Traps and pitfalls abound, so see the *Frantic Formatting* chapter to get through safely.

The Invisible Disk (Drive not ready)

We've all done the invisible disk bit, and if you haven't done it yet, you will sooner or later. You type something like **DIR A:** and then realize that you've forgotten to put a disk in the drive. DOS looks and looks and finally realizes that there's nothing there to read. Then you get this message:

```
Drive not ready error
```

Just put the disk in, this time, and remember to close the drive door before reentering the command.

If there *is* a disk in there and the drive door *is* closed, you may have a disk drive problem. Remove the disk, restart the computer, and try the command again. If the drive *still* isn't ready, it's time to call your witch doctor for a replacement.

Always Have a Backup

How to Make a Backup

The best defense, as they say, is a good offense. The moral? Make copies of important files. Religiously.

DOS has a BACKUP command to help you make safe copies of your files. But be forewarned: You need lots of already-formatted disks (about one high-density disk per megabyte of storage space). When you've got the disks you need, type

```
BACKUP C:\*.* A:
```

and follow the instructions that appear magically on your screen. (If your hard disk is something other than C, substitute its name for C in the preceding line. And if you're backing up to a disk in drive B, replace A with B.)

If it ever really happens that your hard disk grinds to a halt and you lose all your data (it probably won't happen, now that you've got a backup), you may use the RESTORE command to put all those BACKUP files back on your hard disk.

DOS 6.x finally replaced **BACKUP** and **RESTORE** with the far better **MSBACKUP** (and **MWBACKUP** for Windows). This one program handles both file backup and after-crisis restoration. Type **MSBACKUP** and select the Backup option to get things started. MSBACKUP is automatically set to make a full backup of drive C to either floppy drive A: or B: (if you've got one). Do at least one backup with this setting.

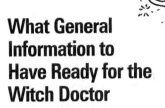

What General Information to Have Ready for the Witch Doctor

Before you begin to talk about your specific problem, the witch doctor may ask you some of the following questions. If you are prepared, it will facilitate the interaction greatly.

- What kind of system are you running (DOS or Macintosh)?
- What version of the operating system (DOS) do you have?
- Are you running Windows or working from DOS alone?
- What applications are you using (Word, Paradox, WordPerfect, Excel)? What versions of the applications software?
- What is your name, department number, serial number for the software, warranty expiration date on your machine, date of purchase, and other identifying information?
- What do you have loaded in your CONFIG.SYS and AUTOEXEC.BAT files?
- Are you logged on to a network while you are experiencing the problem or is it on a stand-alone machine?
- What other peripherals and special devices do you have hooked up to your machine?

When Good Disks Go Bad

Poison: Bad disks

You just used it yesterday. You saved a file out to the disk after you
finished writing that letter to your psychic. Now, when
you try to open the file, you're getting the ARF error.

This is one of those sooner-or-later-it's-going-to-
happen kind of problems. There's no making sense of
it. Something inside the disk just fries, and you're left
with a piece of plastic that's not good for much except
target practice.

Sure you want to know what happened, but first things first:
Can you save the data that was on there?

Better get out the crying towel. Probably not.

Antidote: If you have a disk-recovery utility, such as Norton Disk
Doctor, you can try doing a little diagnostic work on the disk before giving
up. If you don't, you can press R for Retry a couple of
times to see if DOS suddenly wakes up and can read
the file. But you better not count on it. And if the
data is really important, call your witch doctor.

Disk Readin' and Writin'

Most disks don't just go sort-of bad. They go really bad
(sort of like eggs). There's no mistaking what's going on.
You want to save that file. Put the disk in the drive, close the
drive door, and choose the necessary commands.

No way, says DOS.

```
Unrecoverable write error on drive A, side 1, track 29
```

(Your drive letter and numbers will be different, of course, unless it's a really creepy coincidence.) DOS instead might try to tell you

```
Write failure, diskette unusable
```

or perhaps

```
Write fault error
```

Antidote: Before completely panicking, take the disk out and make sure you inserted it correctly. Put it back in and try again. If the error comes up again, continue panicking.

Note: If the disk contains data that's really important, call your witch doctor *before trying anything else.* He may have a special recovery program that reads disks DOS can't. For those of you on your own, try **RESCUE** (one of the best programs available for this sort of crisis).

In any case, that disk is a goner. You can try to reformat (which just means to use FORMAT to erase everything on the disk and start over), but it's probably safer to just throw the thing away.

If you're trying to load a file from a disk that's on its way out, DOS will churn around in the drive for a while before displaying

```
Unrecoverable read error on drive A, side 1, track 29
```

Again, you're looking at a reformat job (at least) or file 13 (that's the trash can). In both cases, you're out of some files, unless you had a copy.

Incompatible Disk Differences

Poison: Helping disks get along

You save that extremely important report out to the disk in drive A. Everything is working normally. You feel confident that you've got the upper hand with your version of DOS and are beginning to think you're in the driver's seat. You carry your disk over to a friend's machine so you can use her snazzy-dazzy inkjet printer.

Smiling, you put the disk in drive A and close the drive door. "I'm going to win an award with this report," you brag.

```
Abort, Retry, Fail?
```

The smile fades. Instead of the ARF error, you might see

```
Drive or diskette types not compatible
```

Antidote: If the disk works on your computer but doesn't on your friend's, you've probably got different density drives. Either you've got high-density and she's got double-density or vice versa. If you really need to print the report on her system, have her format a disk on her machine. Then copy the file over and print it from her machine. Everything should work fine, and all is right with the world.

A Disk Full of Nothing

Poison: Disks full of nothing

You've got only one or two files on a disk. You start to save another file out to the drive, when you see

```
Insufficient disk space
```

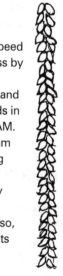

Techie Term

Disk caches can speed up your disk access by reading a little bit ahead on the disk and storing what it finds in some set-aside RAM. When your program asks for something from the disk, the cache may already contain what the program wants. If so, the program gets its info *much* faster

How could your disk be out of space? Take a look and see if you can find out what's going on.

Antidote: It's always a good idea to keep a couple of formatted disks handy, just in case you run up against this error unexpectedly. Then you can pop the disk in the drive, save the necessary files, and store the files away safely without losing any data.

To see what's eating up your disk space, at the DOS prompt, type **CHKDSK /F**. (If the disk you want to check is in drive A, add a space followed by **A:** after the command. For drive B, add **B:** and for the hard disk, **C:**.) If everything's OK technically, DOS scrolls up a half-screenful of information about the disk. Two important items to check are the number of files on the disk and the amount of free space.

If CHKDSK says you've got free space but DOS says the disk is full, check the number of files stored on the disk. If it's pretty high (like over 300), try either erasing or moving a few somewhere else. DOS has a natural limitation (what a surprise!) on the number of files you can store in the root directory of a disk. Once you hit that number, DOS says "the inn is full" regardless of the actual space available.

If CHKDSK finds something amiss, you'll see an error like `lost chains`. This means DOS found some file-pieces cluttering up the disk (usually caused by restarting the computer or sloppy programs). The next line is the ever-popular `Convert chains to files (Y/N)?` question. Type **N** for no and DOS will correct the problem without requiring any further effort from you.

Even though they sound bad, these items aren't anything serious. They are little bits of files strewn about when your computer hiccupped — usually during a sudden power outage or reboot. This information is nothing you need, but it will take up space on your disk you could otherwise use.

If CHKDSK finds lost files, type **CHKDSK** again, but

add **/F** after it. That causes CHKDSK to ask you whether you want to convert the lost chains to files. Type **Y** for Yup.

Type **N** for Nuh-uh and DOS deletes the clusters for you automatically. There. Now you've got more space on your disk.

After you display the CHKDSK information, make sure your printer is ready and press PrtSc. Your printer prints a copy of what was displayed on-screen. Save it and show it to the witch doctor if you have to yell for help later.

Practicing Safe Swapping

Poison: Never take disks from strangers

Some flus are actually caused by a computer virus, which is a terror-inducing word for people in the PC realm. A *virus* is a mean-spirited program that eats away at the data or important processing files on your computer. Not something you'd like to have.

How do you get viruses? Basically two ways:

1. You are using a communications program and downloading files from a public bulletin board system.

2. You're using a disk that was used in other computers.

How do you know you've got one? Call the witch doctor when you see any of the following symptoms:

📟 Your computer shuts down suddenly and displays something weird like *Elmer Fudd for President.*

📟 A bunch of your data disappears suddenly.

📟 You start getting disk read errors on a disk you know is fine.

📟 A program you're quite familiar with suddenly starts behaving errati-cally, or starts singing "Yankee Doodle Dandy" at 5:00.

Antidote:

For best results,
get into the habit of checking any new
files you plan on adding to your hard drive.
Some people recommend virus-checking
preformatted diskettes that you purchase, even if
they are shrink-wrapped.

Disk swapping is one of those perils you learn to
live with — and vaccinate against. Just a few
years ago, we could trade disks with no
particular worries. Today, every disk
is suspect until it's proven innocent.

Viruses are nothing to fool with. Some
viruses won't do anything serious
except display something the
creator — and sometimes *only*
the creator — thinks is
witty. Other viruses can
destroy entire disks —
including massive hard
disks — and spread
unnoticed to other disks and
other systems.

The Protected Disk

Poison: Dealing with write-
protection

Some people like to keep their files
safe by turning on write-protection.

Words of Wisdom:
MSAV and VSAFE

When you receive a new disk, check it with MSAV. Just type MSAV A: /C to seek and destroy any viruses on the disk. DOS also has a full-time virus scanner called VSAFE. I'll probably be called a heretic for this, but unless you're swapping disks like crazy, you probably won't ever run into a computer virus. Let your innate paranoia guide you, but I don't recommend bothering with VSAFE. If virus phobia wins, type **HELP VSAFE** for the entrails — er, details.

SMARTDrive

The DOS 6.2 SMARTDrive supports CD-ROMs in addition to hard disks and floppies. Microsoft even added a new feature to prevent the occasional data loss some people endured with the DOS 6.0 version. SMARTDrive makes sure it's done writing to the disk before sending you back to the DOS prompt.

ScanDisk

Good old venerable CHKDSK is still around, but DOS now includes a much more powerful utility called SCANDISK. If you suspect a disk error, type **SCANDISK**. It does more testing and can repair more intricate problems than its elder cousin. It's a repair utility (and ONLY a repair utility). If you're looking for some informational tidbits, use CHKDSK (without the /F parameter). DoubleSpace uses ScanDisk to check the reliability of your disk before it begins compression.

This means that you can open their files and look at them, but you can't edit or otherwise change them. When you try to change a file on a write-protected disk, you get the rather obvious error

```
Write protect error
```

Antidote: Any way around it? Well, write protection is really something right out of the computer dark ages. When you write-protect a 5.25-inch disk, you put a small tab over the notch on the right side of the disk (that's called the write-protect notch — no surprise there). When you write-protect a 3.5-inch disk, you simply slide the write-protect tab (top left corner) to the up position.

First press A to get out of the error, and then, to remove write-protection, remove the tab or slide the notch down.

Slow Hard Disk

Poison: The computer seems slow when it reads and writes to the hard disk.

Antidote: If an application uses the disk heavily, it's said to be *disk intensive*. You can probably speed things up by using SmartDrive, DOS's free disk caching program (see Words of Wisdom side bar).

Testing the hypothesis:

At the DOS prompt, type **SMARTDRV /S**.

Note: If you see a display babbling about reads, hits, and misses, SmartDrive is already loaded and working. If you still think things are slow, ask your witch doctor to tweak SmartDrive for peak performance.

If lots of things about configuring and installing SmartDrive scroll up the screen, you're on the right track. Type **SMARTDRV** and press Enter. Try your disk-crunching program again. Any difference?

Note: If you don't notice anything, your drive may just *be* slow or perhaps fragmented (see the Words of Wisdom sidebar on DEFRAG for help).

Solving things for good:

If the cache made your drive sing (or at least hum a merry tune), change your AUTOEXEC.BAT file so SmartDrive loads automatically. Just EDIT AUTOEXEC.BAT and add a line that says (ready?) C:\DOS\SMARTDRV.

Note: If you do disk-intensive things all the time, have your witch doctor optimize your cache settings. (Witch doctors *love* to do stuff like that.)

Very Slow Disk

Poison: The disk drive is r e a l l y s l o w and getting s l l o o o o w w w w e r r r.

Antidote: Hmmm . . . sounds like you've got a sloppy hard disk with some seriously fragmented files. If you've got DOS 6.2, don't worry — this is an easy one.

Note: Earlier versions of DOS can't fix fragmented disks by themselves, so you need a program like PC Tools Compress or the Norton Utilities SpeedDisk. See the appropriate documentation for specific help, instructions, and petty amusements.

Small, Small, Smaller Hard Drive

Poison: Ever since you loaded version 143.7a of your favorite application, the hard drive seems small. Really small.

Antidote: The best solution is to buy a bigger hard drive (say around 800MB).

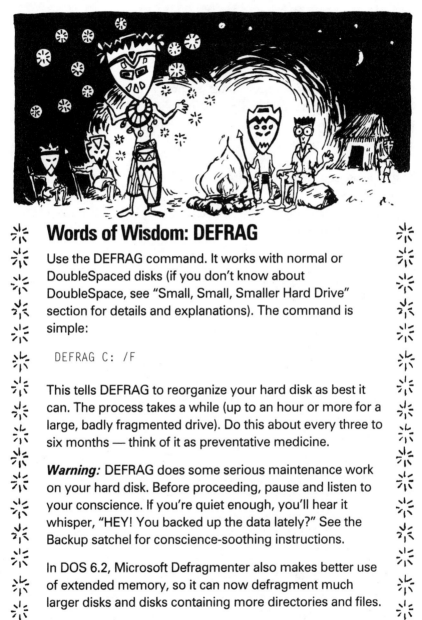

Words of Wisdom: DEFRAG

Use the DEFRAG command. It works with normal or DoubleSpaced disks (if you don't know about DoubleSpace, see "Small, Small, Smaller Hard Drive" section for details and explanations). The command is simple:

```
DEFRAG C: /F
```

This tells DEFRAG to reorganize your hard disk as best it can. The process takes a while (up to an hour or more for a large, badly fragmented drive). Do this about every three to six months — think of it as preventative medicine.

Warning: DEFRAG does some serious maintenance work on your hard disk. Before proceeding, pause and listen to your conscience. If you're quiet enough, you'll hear it whisper, "HEY! You backed up the data lately?" See the Backup satchel for conscience-soothing instructions.

In DOS 6.2, Microsoft Defragmenter also makes better use of extended memory, so it can now defragment much larger disks and disks containing more directories and files.

Unfortunately, you can't always have the best solution. That's why programmers (in their infinite wisdom and never-ending struggle for free disk space to fill) created compression programs.

For the pre-DOS 6 folks, your best bet is a program called Stacker. It's deceptively easy to install, but very powerful and stable. Depending on the files you're storing, Stacker can generally double your disk space. If you have DOS 6.x, you may want to try DoubleSpace.

Warning: Regardless which compression program you use, you're about to perform the software equivalent of gutting your house and rebuilding from the ground up. BACK UP YOUR DATA! (Don't say I didn't warn you!) Call your witch doctor and ask her to install it.

Same Old Disk

Poison: I switched floppy disks but the computer doesn't think I did.

This is a weird problem — it'll give you twilight zone tingles up and down your spine. When you put the first disk in and worked with it, everything was OK. But when you swap disks, the computer acts like the first one is still there. There's no error message, just Rod Serling whispering "Isn't that *weird?*" into your ear.

Antidote: This could be serious, but don't panic yet. Before trying anything else:

- Remove the floppy from the drive.
- If you're in a program, save your work to the hard disk.
- Restart your computer.
- Try your floppy-swap again.

If the problem is gone, odds are it was a "spurious anamoly," but watch for this problem in the future.

If the computer's still acting flaky, do a little more troubleshooting.

Words of Wisdom:
DoubleSpace and DoubleGuard

DOS version 6.x has a built-in compression utility, called *DoubleSpace*, that can squeeze your data into a space half its size. This utility can turn a 40MB hard disk, for example, into something close to an 80MB hard disk. In MS-DOS 6.2, the main emphasis is on enhancements of DoubleSpace. It now includes DoubleGuard safety checking, which protects against data corruption by verifying data integrity before writing data to your disk. You can also easily uncompress a DoubleSpace drive or completely uninstall DoubleSpace. For more information, type `HELP DBLSPACE` at the DOS prompt.

Words of Wisdom: MIRROR

An important disk protection command in DOS 5 and 6.x is MIRROR.

MIRROR saves a copy of the File Allocation Table and root directory in a file called MIRROR.DAT. The UNFORMAT command uses these files. MIRROR also tracks deleted files, making UNDELETEs more reliable. MIRROR should be in your AUTOEXEC.BAT file, so it runs every time your system starts. Pick a line after the PATH statement and put in MIRROR C: /TC.

Maybe your SmartDrive is dumb.

At the DOS prompt, type **SMARTDRV /S**. This tells SmartDrive to display a status report.

Note: If the screen fills with stuff about installing and configuring SmartDrive, go to the next section. SmartDrive isn't running on your computer.

Look at the table labeled "Disk Caching Status." Is there an entry for drive A:? If so, type **SMARTDRV A-** (or **B-** if that's the drive in question). This tells SmartDrive to disable caching for that drive.

Try your floppy swap one more time. If it failed, go on to the "bad news" section. If it finally worked, edit your AUTOEXEC.BAT file and change the first part of the SmartDrive command like this:

```
SMARTDRV A-
```

I'm afraid I have some bad news.

If it's still failing, you're likely dealing with a bad floppy drive or a floppy controller problem. Call your WD and get ready for repair bills.

And tell Rod to be quiet.

Techie Term

Spurious anamoly is a genuine witch doctor term for "a really weird problem that comes from nowhere, hits hard, and vanishes when you restart the computer." Witch doctors think these problems are related to various natural events (I personally linked them to sun spots), but don't know for certain. Individual spurious anamolies cannot be resolved, but recurring SAs (which we call GAs or genuine anamolies) can be fixed. SAs are considered good luck in some parts of the world, although not around here.

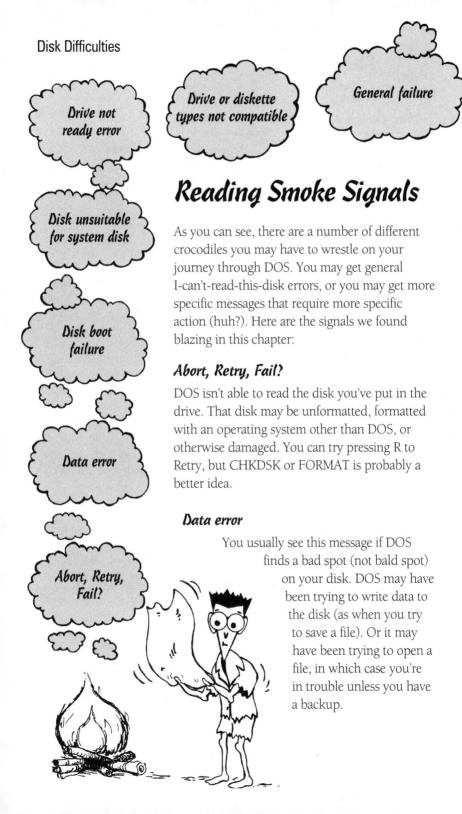

Drive not
ready error

Drive or diskette
types not compatible

General failure

Disk unsuitable
for system disk

Disk boot
failure

Data error

Abort, Retry,
Fail?

Reading Smoke Signals

As you can see, there are a number of different
crocodiles you may have to wrestle on your
journey through DOS. You may get general
I-can't-read-this-disk errors, or you may get more
specific messages that require more specific
action (huh?). Here are the signals we found
blazing in this chapter:

Abort, Retry, Fail?

DOS isn't able to read the disk you've put in the
drive. That disk may be unformatted, formatted
with an operating system other than DOS, or
otherwise damaged. You can try pressing R to
Retry, but CHKDSK or FORMAT is probably a
better idea.

Data error

You usually see this message if DOS
finds a bad spot (not bald spot)
on your disk. DOS may have
been trying to write data to
the disk (as when you try
to save a file). Or it may
have been trying to open a
file, in which case you're
in trouble unless you have
a backup.

The data error message appears holding hands with a companion message:

```
Abort, Retry, Fail
```

If you select R (Retry), DOS may be able to read the bad spot. But don't get your expectations up. Even if DOS can load the file, it may contain strange gobbledygook characters or big holes. It's much safer to use your backup.

Disk boot failure

`Disk book failure` is a Yikes! message. DOS can't load the files it needs to get things started. Leave the message on the screen and set your sights on the nearest technical support person.

Disk unsuitable for system disk

This error means that the disk you've chosen to be your Survival Disk (oh, lucky disk) isn't of the primo quality DOS expects. Not good enough, in other words. It may have a bad spot or two. Choose a different disk for the system disk and use this one to store data files.

Drive not ready error

Guess what? The drive's not ready. Did you close the drive door? Did you put the disk in first?

Drive or diskette types not compatible

Who said DOS was hard to understand? Obviously, the diskette you put in that drive isn't the right type. Remember, you can use high- or double-density disks in a high-density drive, but you can use only double-density disks in a double-density drive.

General failure

This error shows up when DOS knows something isn't working right and doesn't know what. Most likely, you'll see this on a top line with the ARF message or its buddy Abort, Retry, Ignore? underneath.

Insufficient disk space

Ooohhh, you'll hate this one when you get it. Most likely, you'll see this error after you've been working for an hour on a really important document or spreadsheet. You go to save the file, and — sorry. No room on the disk. **Best advice:** Have a couple of spare disks formatted and ready, just in case you get this error.

No room for system on destination disk

Well, you can see this one coming. DOS thinks that if you want to turn that floppy disk into a system disk, it should have first choice about where to put the system files. If the spot DOS wants for the system files is used by something else, DOS crosses its arms and says "Sorry. No can do." Try removing unnecessary files before using FORMAT A:/S or use a different disk.

Non-DOS disk

This appears alongside Abort, Retry, Ignore, Fail. It's telling you that the disk you want DOS to read isn't a disk that's formatted in DOS's language. Did you put a Mac disk in there? Check your disk (is the drive door closed?) and type either **R** for Retry or **A** for Abort. (Don't **I** anything — ignoring problems only makes them worse.)

Not ready, reading drive A

This one is simple. You told DOS to look at drive A (for whatever reason — maybe you were copying a file to the disk in the drive). DOS tried to look

at the drive but found that it couldn't. Possible reasons include the following: You forgot to put the disk in the drive; you really meant to choose drive B; or you didn't close the drive door. Make any necessary adjustments and try the operation again.

Target disk bad or incompatible

Either that disk is a chump or you've got the wrong type. DOS isn't sure which. Take the disk out and put it back in; try the command again. Check to see what kind of disk you've got (a low-density has a ring in the center that a high-density disk does not) or try the disk on another machine to see whether it's the disk itself or the density that's the problem.

Unrecognized disk error

This is another one of those "Hmmmm" kinds of problems. Chances are, your drive and diskette aren't compatible. No, counseling won't help. Do the disk routine: Check the drive door (if you've got one), make sure the disk is inserted properly, rule out any physical problems. Everything okay? Try the disk in another machine and see if you can get a directory. If you continue to get this error in both high- and low-density drives, you've probably got a bad disk.

Unrecoverable write error on drive A, side 1, track 29

This happens when you're trying to save a file out to disk and DOS just can't do it. The diskette is bad. If DOS can't read the disk, the message Unrecoverable read error is displayed.

Write failure, diskette unusable. Or Write fault error

These nasty errors both appear when DOS can't work with the disk you want to use. You can FORMAT the disk or start over with another disk. It probably means that the file allocation table on the disk you're using has gone bad (hopefully, that's not drive C). You may want to just take the disk out (if it's a floppy), dig a hole in the backyard, and bury it. There's no hope.

Write protect error

You tried to bite into a write-protected file. Press A to Abort the operation and then get another disk or remove the write-protection from the current one (using ATTRIB -R).

Things to Do with Dead Disks
- Rip it open and play with the disk part (great stress relief!)
- Loan it to someone who borrows things but never returns them.
- Pin it to your bookcase with a magnet; then say to your office mate, "This disk's been giving me some problems lately."
- Chew on it (why should your pets have all the fun?).
- Use two and make play glasses for your kids.
- Mount it like a trophy and brag about your latest "kill."

You Know You're Really in Trouble When . . .

You get a read or write error on your hard disk

This means that DOS is having some serious trouble figuring out what's going on with the information there. Nothing is being read from the disk, and nothing is being written to the disk. This problem is bad enough on a small 5.25-inch or 3.5-inch disk, but when you're talking about the hard disk, not being able to get to that information is a big deal. Don't mess with anything. Back slowly away from your computer. When you're a safe distance away, start yelling for the witch doctor; you're going to need some technical support.

You put a disk in drive B, type DIR B:, and the light in A goes on

Here's another oddball problem that is not something for us robin scouts to deal with. Something is connected wrong — or is unconnected — inside your system. Get that witch doctor on the phone (or the drums).

A label is stuck in the drive

This may sound silly, but it happens. Don't you hate to pull old labels off? Some users put labels over labels over labels. Pretty soon they have a pile of labels an eighth of an inch thick. It's not entirely impossible that one label (or a portion of one) could wiggle loose and climb back in the drive. If this happens to you, don't go digging around in there with a screwdriver or scissors. Two major things could happen: you could get zapped into Electrical La La Land, or you could ruin the drive forever. Let the witch doctor retrieve the sticky little beast for you.

You get an error message that says something about partitions

When your computer is born, there's nothing on the hard disk. Like any other kind of disk, the hard disk has to be formatted before it can store any information. Having 130MB of nothing is not useful for much of anything.

A small fraction of the population can deal with the emotional trauma and pinpoint pressure of hard-disk formatting. These people understand things like DOS partitions, batch files, and file buffers.

These people are professionals. Don't try this at home.

There may be a number of errors you see that say something about partitions, such as

```
Invalid partition table
```

or

```
Error reading partition table
```

In any case, whenever you see an error message concerning a partition, get someone who knows something over to your system pronto. This problem is not something you can fix yourself. It has something to do with the way your hard disk is set up, which makes it too important to mess with.

Chapter 4 Directory Dangers

Paths through Peril

This chapter leads you up a steep hill to the Temple of DIR.

It may be the most important find on your entire journey. From the underbrush, you can see it, stretching like a Mayan temple against a darkening sky. Carefully you skirt the edges of the overgrown path, trying to keep out of the glow of the tiki lamps.

It's kind of a yellow-brick-road thing . . . or maybe more like a rat in a maze. Well, Psychology lab or not, you're gonna get through this thing.

The sign says something about a temple up ahead. Surely, there will be some clue there as to how to get home again. All you have to do now is find it.

DOS Won't DIR

Poison: DIRs that don't display

You try to get a directory by typing **DIR** at the prompt and pressing Enter. *DOS For Dummies* told you how. But your computer stubbornly displays the following message:

```
Bad command or file name
```

What went wrong? Are you sure you typed the command correctly? Sorry — had to ask. Another, more obvious, error message you may encounter as a result of a typo is

```
Invalid directory
```

Antidote: Stumbling fingers are a common cause of this particular DOS symptom, especially for single-finger DOS typists. It's a simple mistake. And there really is no other explanation for a non-DIRing computer.

Life in the Fast Screen

Poison: File lists that zip by at the speed of light

You type **DIR**, press Enter, and — whoa! What was that? Something scrolled by on your screen so fast it could have said anything. You can see the bottom of the list, showing you the names of a few files and the amount of space used and space available. Not a lot of help when you're looking for something specific.

If the current directory holds only a couple of files, doing a regular DIR is no big deal. Your listing will be just a few lines long, and you'll have all the information you need.

If, however, the directory contains a bunch of files (more than 25, to be exact), the topmost files will scroll off the top of the screen before you get a chance to read them.

Antidote: Here are three solutions:

➥ **Ask for a wide directory listing.** If you add /W to the DIR command (type **DIR /W**), DOS displays the listing across the width of the screen. Unless you have an enormous number of files and directories, you can see all your files on-screen at once.

Techie Term

The word *directory* is a rather vague term for "the place where your files are stored." Think of it this way: If you put three shoe boxes on the floor and pitch baseball cards in one, football cards in another, and hockey cards in the third, you have, in effect, created a BASEBALL directory, a FOOTBALL directory, and a HOCKEY directory.

🕮 **Have DOS pause the display so you can read it.** Add /P (that's slash
P) after the DIR command. This tells DOS to display some files and
then pause so you can take a few seconds to read through them. When
you're finished, you press a key to start the display scrolling again.
Type

```
DIR /P
```

Then press Enter. DOS displays the first 20 or so lines and then
displays the following message:

```
Press any key to continue . . .
```

Read through the list and press any key on the keyboard when you're
done. DOS scrolls the next set of lines onto the screen.

🕮 **You can tell DOS to display almost anything one screenful at a
time by putting |** MORE **after the command.** To see an extensive text
file screen-by-screen:

```
TYPE LONG_ONE.TXT | MORE
```

DOS displays the first screen of information and then shows — MORE
— at the bottom of the screen. When you press a key, DOS displays
the next screen.

My Files Are Lost!

Poison: Can't find your file

Wait — don't panic. Your files probably are in there
somewhere, hiding. When you typed DIR and
pressed Enter, did DOS display something like
this:

```
Volume in drive C is DISK1_VOL1
Volume Serial Number is 2439-0DD8
Directory of C:\
File not found
```

Antidote: If so, you probably entered the command a little squirrelly. (Don't take it personally — DOS is particular when it comes to having commands entered a certain way.)

➡ **Get the right name:** Are you sure there *is* a directory with the name you're entering?

➡ **Get the right PATH:** Is the directory path correct? You can't type **DIR MEAT\SPAM** when you mean **DIR MEAT\MYSTERY\SPAM**

➡ **Remember your roots:** Giving DOS the full path name, starting from the root directory, increases your chances for success.

➡ **When all else fails**, search: If you *still* can't find the directory, but you know at least part of the name of a file in it, use DIR's search option (DIR/S). To find the menu planner directory by looking for last week's menu, type

```
DIR/S MENU*.DOC
```

DOS bumps, grinds, and whirrs your drive for a while but ultimately displays your menus under the heading

```
Directory of
C:\TUPPERWR\COFFINS
```

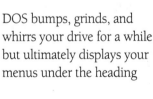

Where'd That Directory Go?

Poison: Overgrown paths

You created a new directory just before lunch and copied your work files over to it. And now you can't find it anywhere. Could it be that your computer really didn't create the directory? Could it be that your files are floating around inside your hard disk somewhere, and you'll never see them again?

Take a deep breath. Probably not.

Working with directories takes a little bit of finesse at first, but after you figure out what you're doing, you learn that nothing really dangerous can happen. A directory is simply a storage space for files, so whether you're creating a directory or removing one, you're only working with the *container*, not the files themselves. (The dangerous stuff happens when you begin erasing files.)

Antidote: You can take several steps to find your way back to familiar territory:

🖚 Get yourself back to recognizable ground by returning to the root directory. Type **CD ** and press Enter.

🖚 If you remember a file name, use DIR/S and let DOS tell you the path. See **"My Files Are Lost!"** for help with searching.

🖚 Use the TREE command to display a diagram of all the directories and subdirectories on your disk. Just make sure you're logged on to the right drive, type **TREE**, and press Enter.

An Un-Make-Able Directory

Poison: Directories that won't create

Creating directories may not seem like an intimidating process, but you can wander off the path into some potential problems.

Suppose you use the MD command to create a directory and press Enter, and DOS says

```
Directory already exists
```

Antidote: There's only one reason for this message: something (a directory or a file) with this name already exists in the path you specified. Use DIR to see what it is. If it's a file, you'll need to delete it before you can recycle the name as a directory.

Note: You can put a file named TWIN into a directory named TWIN, but you can't create a directory C:\TWIN if there's currently a file called C:\TWIN because the name and path are the same.

Identical-Twin Directories

Poison: Directories that show up where you don't expect them

Depending on where you try to create a directory, DOS may not know you're creating a duplicate. That can cause problems for you, your programs, and your data.

Remember how DOS sees its directories? One path at a time. Like this:

```
C:\                       is the root directory.
DIR1    DIR2    DIR3      are our sample directories off C:\.
SDIR1   SDIR2   SDIR3     are the subdirectories of the higher level
                          directories.
```

If C:\ is the current directory, and you try to create another DIR2, DOS sends you a message saying that the directory already exists. If you're in the SDIR2 directory, however, and you enter **MD DIR2**, DOS creates another DIR2 directory underneath SDIR2. The diagram then looks like this:

```
C:\                       is the root directory.
DIR1    DIR2    DIR3      are sample directories off C:\.
SDIR1   SDIR2   SDIR3     are subdirectories of the higher level directories.
DIR2                      is the added subdirectory.
```

Words of Wisdom: Thousands separators

Just to show us that they really do care about the way we strain to read the amount of free space we've got on disk, Microsoft has added thousands separators to the bytes free line that appears in version 6.2 when you type DIR (or MEM, CHKDSK, or FORMAT). Now, at the bottom of that DIR display, instead of a cryptic

```
16139904 bytes free
```

you see

```
16,139,904 bytes free
```

Ahhhh. Much better.

This setup will lead to a lot of confusion and make it pretty difficult to keep track of programs and data. Files are going to get lost or, at least, put in the wrong place.

Antidote: You can do several things once you realize this has happened (and you can do several things to prevent it from happening, too):

🖙 Be sure to use unique names for your subdirectories.

🖙 Use the TREE command to display a diagram of your directories from time to time. That way you can make sure you're not duplicating yourself.

🖙 If you're using DOS 5.0 or earlier, find out which duplicate files you don't need by using the COMP command to compare the files and see which are the most current. Here's how:

```
COMP FILE1 FILE2
```

DOS will compare FILE1 with FILE2 and tell you what's different about the files. If you want to compare an entire subdirectory of files, substitute the paths (such as C:\FIRSTDIR and C:\SECONDIR) for the file names.

🖙 If you've got DOS 6.0 or later, use the FC (File Compare) to find out which files are keepers. Again, the method is simple:

```
FC FILE1 FILE2
```

How to Make Your Directory Life Less Difficult

A pretty simple but super-cool trick of the DOS masters: Use redirection to send your directory list to the printer.

Use the CD command to move to the directory you want to print. Type **DIR > LPT1** (or whatever port your printer is on). The ">" symbol tells DOS to take whatever the command to the left (DIR in this case) would normally send to the screen and send it to wherever we specify on the right. DIR > PRN will also work.

In the unlikely event you'd ever want a *file* with a copy of a directory (for documentation purposes), substitute a file name for the LPT1. For instance: DIR > MY_STUFF.DIR creates a file called MY_STUFF.DIR which contains the output of the DIR command. Is this slick or what?

These copies of your directory contents will really come in handy later if you have a major hard disk problem and need to know what used to be there. They are also handy just to reference. Sometimes, when you see printouts for your directories, you begin to see all the junk in there that should be deleted.

There are some really cool shareware utilities for dealing with disks and directories. Find a witch doctor who has a copy of *DOS 6 SECRETS* (IDG, 1993) and ask him to tell you about LCD, Cleanup, HDIRPLUS, and others.

What Stuff to Have Ready for the Witch Doctor

When the witch doctor arrives and sees that you have the contents of your satchel all ready for him, he will be pleased. Not to mention the fact that he might even be equipped now to solve your problem. All of these items that you have been collecting on your journey and carrying around with you are finally going to pay off:

- A written copy of any error messages that you received
- Printouts of your CONFIG.SYS and AUTOEXEC.BAT files
- Notes you made about the problem
- MSD printout from your system
- Printouts of important directories
- Your system disk and your startup disk
- Backups of files, if applicable
- Application master disks, if applicable
- The manuals for your hardware and software
- Any third-party books you have on the topic
- A bag of snack food (always applicable)

🔶 Once you determine which files (or directories) are the unnecessary ones, you can delete the files (using DEL) or remove the entire directory (using DELTREE).

🔶 If you're still lost (but making good time), call your witch doctor. They're like AAA road service for confounding paths.

Too Darn Many Directories

Poison: There are 237 files in a whole branch of subdirectories, and they all need to go.

Antidote: Get ready for some serious use of DEL and RD. Start anywhere you want and go through these steps:

🔶 CD into a directory to kill.

🔶 DEL *.* to trash all the files therein.

🔶 DIR to see if there are directories "under" this one.

🔶 If there are, pick one and start the process again.

🔶 If not, **CD..** and type **RD** and the directory name.

Done *ad infinitum, ad nauseum*, you'll eventually work your way through the whole sordid mess. Good luck and good sawing.

DELTREE Dilemma

Poison: DELTREE trashed a directory you wanted to keep, and UNDELETE won't help get it back.

Antidote: I hope you have Windows (and installed the DOS 6.2 Windows programs!) because Microsoft left you a present: Undelete for Windows.

This command is *only* available from DOS 6.

In their infinite (or is that finite?) programming wisdom, Microsoft's Windows Undelete *can* restore deleted subdirectories, but the DOS UNDELETE can't.

Go figure.

Words of Wisdom: DELTREE

Those of you with the latest, greatest DOS have DELTREE at your disposal. This is the DOS equivalent of a tactical nuclear weapon and should be treated with the same degree of respect.

To nuke a directory and all its files and branch subdirectories, simply type **DELTREE** and the name of the lucky directory. After answering "Y" to DELTREE's version of the famous "Are you sure?," your directory, its files, and sundry subdirectories are gone.

Warning: Take *great* care when using DELTREE. You can kill your *whole hard drive* (I mean *every* directory, *every* file, *everything* on your drive) with ONE errant DELTREE command. To prevent this:

- Never use DELTREE with wildcards (particularly *.*).

- Always type the explicit path for the target subdirectory (if it's C:\CROSHAIR\TARGET, then type **DELTREE C:\CROSHAIR\TARGET** — take no shortcuts!).

- Feel free to use the old-fashioned CD/DEL/RD commands for directory pruning.

Forging a Path Statement

Path is an innocent-sounding word, isn't it? Who knew it masked such mystery, such potential for disaster?

If you don't understand paths, you'll be forever putting yourself in directories you don't want and saving files in far-off places where you'll never find them again.

A path is a way to give directions to DOS. With the *path statement,* you tell DOS where to get a file or put a file, which directory (or subdirectory) to move to, and where to find the files for a particular program.

Hey — I need my 3-D glasses for this next part. Get them for me, will you? They're in my office, on the bookcase, on the third shelf. That's:

```
OFFICE\BOOKCASE\SHELF3
```

Hmmm. Is this path stuff any clearer now?

When you tell DOS (or any other program) the path to a specific file, you're explaining where and how to look for the file. For example, if you use the path C:\WORD\REPORTS\FROGGIE.DOC, you're saying:

1. Look on drive C.

2. Go to the WORD directory.

3. Then go to the REPORTS subdirectory.

4. And find the file FROGGIE.DOC.

Any time you get a File not found error message, look carefully at your path statement. When a program can't find something that should be there, think about *where* you're telling the program to look. Maybe that's the problem.

Can You Get There from Here?

Poison: Missing directories

Suppose you're in the CLIPART subdirectory of the FRUMP directory on drive C. In other words, you're at

```
C:\FRUMP\CLIPART
```

You decide you want to move to the UTIL directory. You know that the command for changing to another directory is CD, so you type

```
CD UTIL
```

and press Enter. DOS says

```
Invalid directory
```

Oh no, it's not. You know the directory is there — you just used it a few minutes ago.

Antidote: The problem is that you didn't enter the path statement telling DOS how to get to the UTIL directory. To be extra clear, you can enter the complete path, like this:

```
CD C:\UTIL
```

Or, if you want to show DOS quickly how to get to that directory, you can type

```
CD \UTIL
```

If all you need to do is move up one level, you can type

```
CD..
```

That command moves you from the C:\FRUMP\CLIPART subdirectory to the C:\FRUMP directory.

Un-Delete-able Directories

Poison: Directories that won't delete

You decide you're not going to use that old version of Frump Paint anymore, and you want to delete the program and the directory to free up some storage space.

Seems like a reasonable request.

You learned in *DOS For Dummies* that the command for removing directories is RD. So far, so good. While you're in the FRUMP directory, you type **RD FRUMP** and press Enter. DOS scratches its head and says

```
Invalid path, not directory,
or directory not empty
```

Antidote: This message could mean a number of things:

📨 Either the path you entered for the directory doesn't exist, or you forgot to enter a path at all.

➽ The directory you want to delete isn't a directory, or you forgot to specify a directory.

➽ The directory still contains files.

Actually, if you try to delete a directory by using the RD command as just described, all three problems exist. Here's how to delete a directory the *right* way:

1. Delete all files in the directory you want to remove. (Use the ERASE or DEL commands — and make backups first, if necessary. See *DOS For Dummies* for more about deleting files.)

2. Change to the directory one level above the one you want to delete. In this case, you would change to C:\, because FRUMP is a directory off the root.

3. Type **RD**, a space, and the name of the directory you want to delete. (In this case, you'd type **RD FRUMP**.) Then press Enter.

Warning: What? DOS won't let you delete all files in the directory? You get an Access denied error message? What DOS is telling you, in its own blunt manner, is that for some reason, some files in the directory are marked read-only. That means you can look at the files, but you can't change or delete them.

You can change this setting (supervision recommended) by using the ATTRIB command, which changes the attributes of the file. (That's a fancy way of saying that if you use it correctly, the command removes the read-only protection.) In the directory, type **ATTRIB -R,** the path (with the file name), and press Enter. You should then be able to delete the file. And next time you're at the swimming hole together, ask the witch doctor why those files were read-only in the first place.

Note: You can remove a subdirectory without being right there beside it, but you need to make sure you've got your path right. If you want to delete a faraway directory (assuming you already removed the files), enter the full path name after the RD command, like this:

```
RD C:\FRUMP\CLIPART
```

Never a Shortcut When You Need One

Poison: You can't get to the directory you want from where you are.

When you're just learning about directories, getting from one faraway place to another faraway place via the root directory is more than the average bear can stand. Suppose your prompt says

```
C:\WP60\WP6DOCS\PROJECT23\RESEARCH
```

You're pretty far in there. And, because you want to use some of your research data in a presentation you're preparing, you've got to get to some far-off subdirectory of POWERPNT (but you're not sure which one).

Antidote: The simple way to solve this? Type **CD ** and press Enter. You're at least back to a familiar starting point: the root directory. Now you can do a TREE of the root by typing **TREE** and pressing Enter (or move to the subdirectory you know you need and then do TREE). Find the subdirectory and use CD to move to it.

Uncooperative CDs

Poison: DOS won't make the change.

You're looking for Word. You know it's on this computer somewhere. You do a couple of quick DIRs to find the program — ah, here it is. You enter the CD command to change to the right directory, press Enter, and . . .

DOS doesn't move.

Oh, sure, it blinked, but your DOS prompt still shows the root directory of drive C.

Antidote: Were you trying to change to a different drive? If you have a drive C and drive D, for example, and while C:\> is displayed, you type

```
CD D:\WORD\BOOK
```

meaning, of course, to change to the BOOK subdirectory on drive D, DOS pauses for a moment and then displays the same thing you saw before:

```
C:\>
```

What's going on? Try switching over to drive D by typing

```
D:
```

and pressing Enter. DOS shows you that it was, in fact, working, even though you didn't see what was happening. DOS changed to the directory you wanted on drive D. The problem was that you were logged on to C.

Dot and Dot-Dot

Poison: You can't get rid of those blasted dot and dot-dot subdirectories.

You've been studying your handy DOS guide carefully. You know that before you can delete a directory, all files and subdirectories must be removed. But when you try to remove those two ever-present and apparently useless directories, . and . . , nothing happens. They just won't go. How in the world will you ever remove them?

Antidote: You don't need to. They are present only to annoy you and to help DOS remind itself of the current and next-level-up directories. Maybe a better question is "Why are you trying to delete them?" They won't get in the way of your RD directory removal. If you're getting a Directory not empty error, there must be another file or subdirectory in there somewhere. Use DIR to find out.

The Directory That Wouldn't Die

Poison: I've tried everything, and this directory just won't go away.

You check and see what could be keeping this directory on life-support systems. It's not those dot-dot directories. Must be some Big Dark Secret no one has told you about.

Antidote: Maybe you've got some hidden files. Type **DIR /A** and press Enter. All files, including the system files and any hidden files, appear in the directory list. Changing a hidden file to a visible file involves changing a file's attributes (which you do using the ATTRIB command). After you unhide it, you can delete it. But ask the witch doctor first — the file is probably hidden for a reason.

Making Sense of the DIR List

Poison: Lost in DIR

You used DIR /W to display a wide directory list and now you can't tell which things are files and which are directories. All the names are lumped together — with no extensions, file sizes, or dates — so all your usual clues have been hidden from you.

Antidote: You must be using a DOS ancestor pre-5.0. With 5.0 and later, DOS adorned directory

Techie Term

An *attribute* is a special characteristic of a file that you set intentionally. For example, if you want to protect a file and make it read-only (so that it can't be changed), you can add the read-only attribute. If you want to keep a file from being displayed in a file list, you can add the hidden file attribute.

names with the square brackets [and]. This means that the WORD
directory looks like

```
WORD
```

in a wide directory list of DOS 4.0 but looks like

```
[WORD]
```

in a version 5.0 (and later) display. The only real answer? If this problem
gives you a serious pain — and you're dead-set on using the DOS prompt
— upgrade to a newer DOS. If you just want some workable way of
knowing what you've got where, use the DOS Shell or Microsoft Windows.
They give you a much clearer way to tell the directories from the files.

I Just Turned My Back for a Minute . . .

Poison: Now-they're-here, now-they-aren't files

You used a DOS command while you were working in a program, and
now you can't find your files. Okay, who's got the hidden camera? You
thought you'd try something a little daring, and now you're paying for it.

Antidote: Many programs give you the option of running a quick DOS
command or even leaving the program temporarily and returning to the
DOS prompt. There's usually some kind of command in the File menu —
like MS-DOS Command, Run DOS, or Exit to DOS — that enables you to
do what you need to do.

There will be those times when you need to format a disk, copy a file, find
something, or delete unnecessary files while you're working on something
else. Having an easy way to get to DOS and do that simple command —
instead of having to save your file and exit the program first — can be a real
DOS blessing, once you learn how to use it.

Remember that the DOS commands you use affect the program you're working with. When you use the CD command to change the current directory and then return to your program, your program sees the directory you changed to (in your shell out session) as the current directory.

To fix the problem, just check your path. (Depending on your program, it should appear in something akin to an Open Files dialog box.) You can change the directory in your program or, if you prefer, you can shell back out to DOS and use CD to change the directory back to the one you need.

Slow-Moving Directories

Poison: Molasses-like displays

When you try to display a directory list, DOS sits for a real long time before displaying anything. The time it takes to load a file when you're working with a program is longer, too, than it used to be.

Antidote: Better take a look at the directory (or directories) you're using. Have you been mixing program files and data files? Are your important Microsoft Word files — like WORD.EXE and WORD_DCA.EXE — jumbled in the same directory with LETTER.DOC, MEMO1.DOC, and MOM.DOC?

The more files DOS has to wade through in order to find program files (usually the ones that end with EXE), the slower everything is going to work.

The moral? Have a separate DATA subdirectory to store the files you create with your program. Let the program files have their privacy. (This approach also makes it easier — and less dangerous — when you go to clean up the directory later.)

One False Move

Poison: Putting the wrong stuff in the wrong place

You accidentally put a bunch of files in the wrong subdirectory. In fact, you created the subdirectory in the wrong place. What can you do?

Antidote: If you're using a version of DOS pre-6.0, you're stuck with copying the files to the directory you meant to put them in originally and then going back to the old files and deleting them (and the directory too, if it's in the wrong place). If you're using DOS 6.0 or later, you can use the MOVE command.

To MOVE files from one place to another, first use CD to change to the directory where the files are stored. Then type something similar to this:

```
MOVE C:\FROMHERE\*.* C:\TOTHERE
```

DOS then moves all the files (that's the *.*) in the FROMHERE subdirectory to the TOTHERE subdirectory. If you want to get rid of FROMHERE, use the RD command to do the trick.

No Sudden Moves

Poison: Files that disappear after MOVEs

You used MOVE to move files from one directory to another, but some of the files in the second directory are missing now. They were there just a minute ago. What happened?

Antidote: MOVE can bring about big results. Better to take a minute and double-check what you're about to do:

📖 Look carefully at the contents of the directory you're moving from and the directory you're moving to.

📖 Check for identical file names used in both directories.

🦇 Make sure you've got a current backup of all files that will be affected.

🦇 Use TREE to be sure you're not creating a duplicate directory.

When you're reasonably sure everything is safe, proceed carefully. But keep that fire extinguisher nearby . . . just in case.

Let's all breathe a collective sigh of relief: DOS 6.2 brings with it a safety net that says "Are you sure you want to do this?" when you start to move files into a subdirectory that will cause other files to be overwritten.

When you move files from one directory to another, any files in the receiving directory that have the same names as the incoming files will be overwritten. Gone forever.

A really good witch doctor might be able to salvage something of your files. Better get something good for the offering, though.

The Top Five Directory Devils

When you're working with the directories on your disk and you're just not getting the results you want, try these things first:

1. Make sure you spelled the directory name correctly.

2. Make sure you're looking on the right disk.

3. Make sure you're in the right directory.

4. Find the directory you want by using the TREE command or by looking at the diagram in the DOS Shell.

5. Make sure that the directory does, in fact, exist.

Directories aren't so bad after all, are they? Your files are still there, somewhere. You just have to find them, either by using the DIR or TREE commands or by looking at your directories in the DOS Shell.

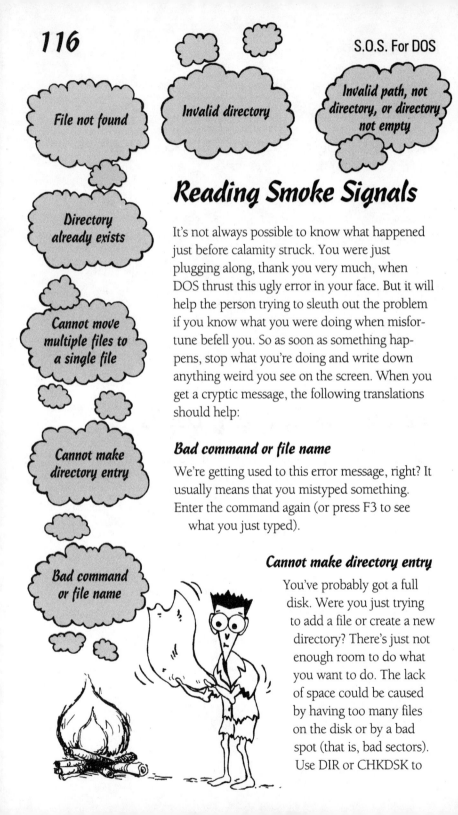

File not found

Invalid directory

Invalid path, not directory, or directory not empty

Directory already exists

Cannot move multiple files to a single file

Cannot make directory entry

Bad command or file name

Reading Smoke Signals

It's not always possible to know what happened just before calamity struck. You were just plugging along, thank you very much, when DOS thrust this ugly error in your face. But it will help the person trying to sleuth out the problem if you know what you were doing when misfortune befell you. So as soon as something happens, stop what you're doing and write down anything weird you see on the screen. When you get a cryptic message, the following translations should help:

Bad command or file name

We're getting used to this error message, right? It usually means that you mistyped something. Enter the command again (or press F3 to see what you just typed).

Cannot make directory entry

You've probably got a full disk. Were you just trying to add a file or create a new directory? There's just not enough room to do what you want to do. The lack of space could be caused by having too many files on the disk or by a bad spot (that is, bad sectors). Use DIR or CHKDSK to find out what's what, and then delete any unnecessary files before trying to add anything else to the disk.

Cannot move multiple files to a single file

DOS 6.0 will let you rename a file after you move it. You tell DOS

```
MOVE C:\FROMHERE\THISFILE C:\TOTHERE\THATFILE
```

And DOS moves THISFILE, renames it to THATFILE, and puts it in the TOTHERE directory. But if you try to move more than one file and specify a new name (you can MOVE more than one file, but you can't rename more than one file while you're MOVEing), DOS thinks you're trying to put more than one file into the THATFILE file.

Directory already exists

DOS rules say that you can't create two directories with the same name on the same level. You're trying to create a directory that already exists.

File not found

This is another one of those DOS "Huh?" messages. DOS says, "Are you sure that's what you mean? I can't find anything like that." Are you sure you're in the right directory? Are you looking on the right drive? *Is* there a directory with the name you're entering? Are you sure that you typed the name of the file correctly? Did someone (gulp) delete the file? Check your spelling and your directory; then try again.

Invalid directory

DOS is seeing something in the command that it doesn't recognize as a directory. The problem could be a typo. You may be trying to change to a different directory using the CD command or remove a directory with the RD command. It could be that you're not in the right directory (or on the right drive). Look at the prompt to see whether you are where you're supposed to be. Then issue the command again.

Invalid path, not directory, or directory not empty

Chances are, you're trying to remove a directory that's not empty. Change to the directory (use CD) and display a listing (use DIR) to find out. Remember to move to the level above the one you want to delete before you use the RD command. Entering the complete path name (C:\FRUMP\CLIPART) is always a good idea when you're removing things.

You Know You're Really in Trouble When . . .

Minutes after you erase all your WordPerfect program files and delete the directories, your boss asks for a report you did six months ago

Undelete's not going to save you now. Time for some creative thinking. And, if you catch your witch doctor in a good mood, you might benefit from a few magic utilities that could save at least part of your data.

You try to display a TREE of drive D and get a read error

Uh-oh. Try again, typing the command carefully. No luck? Because you can't be sure exactly what is going bad, don't press anything or turn anything off (they'll be able to lift your fingerprints later). Be prepared to plead with the nearest tech support person for insight as to what to do next.

Finally, under a dark, terrifying sky, you find the mysterious temple, with natives standing guard. And then, suddenly, the first true face-to-face with the revered and ominous witch doctor!

Part II

Where Do I Go Now?

Uh oh! The natives are starting to chase you. But you hadn't meant any harm. Maybe they're mad that you found their sacred temple. No time for chitchat though. Better run now and explain later.

Chapter 5

File
Fiascoes

Paths through Peril

One of the biggest keys to dealing with file problems is to keep your cool. If you can't find a file or a file turned to mush while you slept, don't panic. That's just what the Venus Filetraps want, you know: to scare you and send you running hysterically into the forest. Don't fall for it.

Arrggg! I Needed That File!

If you're like most people, you get in a disk-cleaning frenzy every few weeks. Depending on how often you use your computer and how many files you create, your hard disk and diskettes can get pretty full pretty fast. And it's so simple to go zipping through the directories, deleting all the old files you don't need anymore.

And then —

What was that? Did you just press Y when DOS asked you to confirm that you wanted to delete all files in the directory? Was that the *root* directory?

Words of Wisdom: Backups

It bears repeating at least six different ways that one cannot overemphasize the importance of making regular backups of your important files. Ask any technical support person, and he or she will tell you time and time again, in countless situations, "This would not have been a problem if you had made a backup." If you're lucky, you have a network administrator who makes nightly backups of all of your data on the network. Even then, there are many times when losing even four hours of work can be a disaster. The key is that there is more than time lost — there's energy. And sometimes creative energy (like when you're "composing at the terminal") only wants to visit you once.

Whether you deleted just one important file or a whole slew of them, you can use the Undelete feature to bring the data back from the Land of the Lost.

Undelete is available only with DOS version 5.0 and up. If you have an earlier version, you need to use another utility program, such as Norton Utilities, to get Undelete.

To use Undelete, move to the directory that contained the file(s) you just deleted. Type **UNDELETE** and press Enter. DOS loads the Undelete utility and displays some information, including a request about whether to undelete a file.

If you type **Y**, DOS says

```
Please type the first character for ?E          .DOC:
```

(The name of your file will, of course, be different.) Type the character and DOS tells you

```
File successfully undeleted.
```

Whew! That was a close one.

Undelete works best when you catch the mistake soon after you make it. For example, if you delete a file accidentally on Tuesday and don't discover the mistake until Friday, after creating and deleting a number of files on Wednesday and Thursday, you may have trouble recovering the file.

It Was There a Minute Ago!

You're looking for a specific file. You know it's in there; you were just working with it before lunch. But when you try to copy the file from one directory to another, DOS says

```
Bad command or file name
```

It may seem incredible, but the single biggest reason files disappear — or rather, *seem* to disappear — is Finger Confusion. Did you type those letters in the right order? Press F3 to find out.

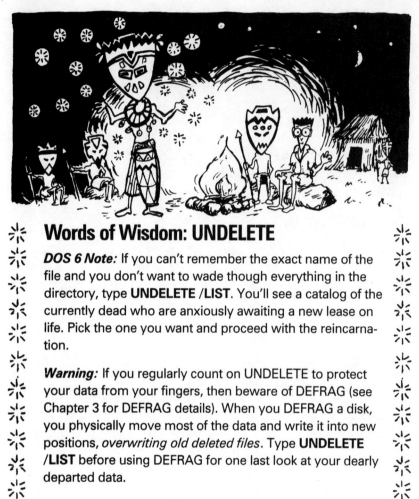

Words of Wisdom: UNDELETE

DOS 6 Note: If you can't remember the exact name of the file and you don't want to wade though everything in the directory, type **UNDELETE /LIST**. You'll see a catalog of the currently dead who are anxiously awaiting a new lease on life. Pick the one you want and proceed with the reincarnation.

Warning: If you regularly count on UNDELETE to protect your data from your fingers, then beware of DEFRAG (see Chapter 3 for DEFRAG details). When you DEFRAG a disk, you physically move most of the data and write it into new positions, *overwriting old deleted files*. Type **UNDELETE /LIST** before using DEFRAG for one last look at your dearly departed data.

What Am I Doing Wrong?

You spelled everything correctly when you typed in your file name. And yet you still see that unfriendly message

```
File not found
```

The second most popular reason people think their files are lost is — show us the board, Don Pardo! — they're looking in the wrong directory.

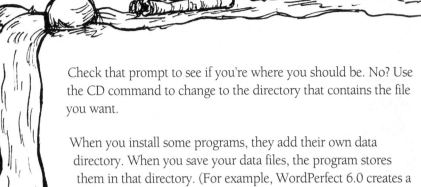

Check that prompt to see if you're where you should be. No? Use the CD command to change to the directory that contains the file you want.

When you install some programs, they add their own data directory. When you save your data files, the program stores them in that directory. (For example, WordPerfect 6.0 creates a WPDOCS directory to store files you create.) You may not know about the directory because you didn't create it in the first place. When you're looking for missing files, use the TREE command or display the DOS Shell to see all the subdirectories in a particular directory.

Can a File Disappear?

Seventy-two percent of people surveyed have had a file vanish into thin air. If this happens to you, there are only three explanations:

1. You are a victim of professional espionage.

2. Your computer is not really your computer at all but a brilliantly disguised replica meant to fool you into entering important data into it.

3. Don't take this personally, but maybe (just maybe) you accidentally deleted the file.

If you tried retyping the command and changing to the right directory and you still can't find the file, try using UNDELETE (see **"ARRGGG! I needed That File!"** earlier in this chapter).

Beware of Falls

That Disk Ate My Files!

Poison: The-file-of-my-heart is on the-disk-in-the-trash

Antidote: We've talked about this before. To briefly recap:

- Floppy disks die (it is the way of things).

- When they die, they take your data with them (snivelling, cowardly little things that they are).

- Don't store anything original that you care about on a floppy.

See Chapter 3 for the lecture text and full conference proceedings on this topic.

If you keep all your Important Files on a diskette that you use day after day after day, you're a gambler. Sooner or later, that disk is going to say, "That's it — I'm pooped" and give up. If you don't have a backup copy of the disk, you're going to be in Big Trouble.

Disks can throw in the proverbial towel for a number of reasons. One reason has more to do with files than the disk itself. That reason is FAT.

When you're working in a program and want to save a file to the disk in drive A, for example, the process starts with DOS looking in the file allocation table. "Where do I have room to store this file?" it wonders. Then it writes the information to the disk and keeps track of the data's location by making an entry in the FAT.

Some people, unaware of the magic going on, swap disks midstream. They save the file to one disk in drive A and then swap disks so they can save the file to another disk in drive A. The problem is that the second disk has a different FAT, which can spell trouble. When the big one hits, it announces itself in the following way:

```
Write failure, diskette unusable
```

If you get this message, your disk is toast. Throw it out and start again. (Good reason for backing up, right?)

To be on the safe side of FAT, be careful how you swap disks during normal operation. For best results, log on to the new disk before you try saving information to it.

FAT Problems (Or When Good Allocation Tables Go Bad)

The FAT is a pretty high-end, technoid-type problem, so we won't waste much more time on it. Remember, however, that if you get the error

```
File allocation table bad,
drive c:
```

it's a pretty serious message. DOS is telling you that it can't read the file allocation table on your hard disk, which is cause for some alarm.

It's probably nothing you did. People can do many mean things to their computers, but messing up the FAT from the DOS prompt usually isn't one of them. Viruses? Maybe. Bad spots on the disk? Likely. Typing **DIR** at the wrong time? No.

The odds are that you'll never know what caused the error. That's just the way the little buggers are. Accept the loss and rejoin regularly scheduled life (already in progress). In any case, if you see something suspicious and it involves your hard disk, grab a witch doctor as quickly as possible.

Techie Term

It's hard to believe, in our weight-conscious society, that FAT is as important to a disk as data is to your programs. *FAT* is actually an acronym for *file allocation table,* which is like an index DOS uses to find out what files are stored where.

But That's Not How I Left It . . .

Yesterday, you wrote Zoe a memo about your upcoming vacation to the Orient and your request to take a few extra vacation days. When you talked to her on the phone this morning, she hadn't received it.

You start your word processing program and open the file MEMO.DOC, intending to print memo again. But instead of the memo to Zoe, you find a memo to Mrs. Pickles, your son's kindergarten teacher. How did one file turn into another? You open all your different files in the directory, but none of them produce the Zoe memo.

Here's the best reason in the world for using unique file names: Your memo to Zoe disappeared because you gave the Mrs. Pickles file the same name as you gave the Zoe file. The Mrs. Pickles memo overwrote the Zoe memo.

Sigh.

It's easy to forget about file-naming conventions when you're just dashing off a quick
memo. So here are a few hints:

- Always try to include in the
  file name something
  unique that

reflects the file's content. For example, you could have named the first memo ZOE.DOC and the second MEMPIK.DOC. Those few characters would have jogged your memory and kept you from overwriting something you needed.

 Come up with your own file-naming conventions. You learned from *DOS For Dummies* that DOS lets you use only eight characters as the root part of the file name (and the three-letter extension is used by most programs, although you can change it if you like). Decide how you'll treat memos, reports, letters, spreadsheets, and other stuff and then write your conventions down and pin them on your bulletin board.

Warning: BIG WARNING!!! If you save, copy, or otherwise write one file on top of another using the same name, briefly go through these three simple steps:

 Look at your data

 Raise your hand

 Wave good-bye

You cannot recover a file overwritten by another with the same name. Let me say that again, with emphasis: you CANNOT EVER recover an overwritten file. It's gone for good and left no forwarding address.

Tell Me Again — What's File Amnesia?

Ten minutes ago you could remember the name of that file. If only your boss hadn't asked you for it, you'd surely be able to find it now. You sit at your desk with your head in your hands, trying to remember the name of that gosh-darn file. File amnesia.

Don't worry; the following sections contain some ideas to help jog your memory.

Directory sleuthing

Let's narrow it down:

➥ What program were you using when you created the file? Change to that directory.

➥ When you named the file, did you follow the conventions you created in the last section? (OK, I won't be unreasonable.)

➥ Does the program directory have a subdirectory where all the data files are stored?

If you remember part of the file name but not where the file is stored, you can use the DIR command with /S to search all directories for the characters you enter. For example, to search for all files that start with the letters *IDG*, you type **DIR \IDG*.* /S**.

Viewing file contents

When you get to the directory you need (or the one you *suspect* you need), you see dozens of files that all look alike. If you haven't given your files unique names, you may be in for a long search process.

When you find a file that may be the one you want, use the TYPE command to display the contents of the file. If the file is a long one, use | MORE to pause the display so it doesn't go hog-wild and scroll itself off the screen.

Many programs have built-in file management capabilities. If yours has such tools, take a minute and learn about them. It's a lot easier than trying to browse a Microsoft Word document from the DOS prompt.

How about a date?

Another way you can find a particular file is to check for the date it was created or last modified. When you request a directory listing (by typing **DIR** and pressing Enter), DOS lists the files in single-column form, such as in the following:

```
STORY      DOC      2560      11-15-93      10:20a
```

This list tells you several things: the name of the file; the size (in bytes) of the file; the date the file was created or last changed; and the time it was saved. Sure, you've got three STORYs. But which one did you create in the evening? What about during work time? Winter, spring, or fall? And the night of November 15th — what were you doing up so late?

Written in Stone: The Unchangeable File

The people who invented write-protection no doubt thought they were doing the rest of us a service by protecting us from ourselves. Write-protection keeps you from accidentally saving information to a disk that shouldn't be changed. The people who created the disk want it to stay just the way it is, thank you very much. And they tell you so by displaying a message like

```
Access denied
```

or

```
Write protect error
```

When disks are write-protected, something physical is changed so you can't write data to the disk. On

Techie Term

Individual files can also be protected from change. These files are called *read-only* files, meaning that DOS will only allow you to read the contents of the file. You can't modify what you find there. For the most part, if you encounter a read-only file, believe that someone protected the file for a reason and leave it alone.

If you need to delete the file or move it to another directory, you first have to remove the read-only setting (don't panic — it doesn't involve surgery). To do so, change to the directory that contains the file, type **ATTRIB -R** and the file name, and press Enter. You then should be able to delete the file.

5.25-inch diskettes, it's a tab; on 3.5-inch disks, it's a switch. If you're working in a program and try to save a file to a write-protected disk, chances are you'll get a beep and some kind of you-don't-want-to-do-that message.

Warning: If someone took the time to make a file read-only, you should think three or four times about deleting it. Granted, maybe you never heard of ETHDRV.SYS, but it's better to ask before trashing it. If your choice is feeling kinda silly by asking versus demonstrating advanced mind-numbness by acting, I'd ask.

The Scrambled File

It's one of the unexplainable things about working with computers: Sometimes weird stuff happens. You open a word processing file expecting to see your quarterly report, and you find part of your novel mixed in among the statistics. You're reading through the research paper you're preparing to hand in, and you find that the last two pages are nothing but odd characters that make no sense at all.

You've been scrambled.

No one is really sure how and why data jumps around inside your computer and sticks where it doesn't belong. The problem could be caused by a number of things:

- Is your system near anything magnetic (besides your personality)? Data doesn't do well around magnetic fields.

- Is the storage space on your disk almost gone? If so, DOS may be searching for places to store your file and may actually scatter it in several places on the disk. You won't be aware of this until you get an error message.

- Did you run CHKDSK /F lately? This DOS command finds lost chains of data that are scattered around your disk and puts them back together.

For more information about CHKDSK (and ScanDisk from DOS 6.2), see Chapter 3.

If your data is scrambled together, you can't do a lot about it. You can go in, edit out the garbage, and reenter the data you need, but there's no easy way to undo what's been done. Of course, if you made that backup, you can just get your handy copy of the file and blow the corrupted one away. . . .

Files Full of Gunk

Poison: Close encounters of the worst kind

You were trying to view the contents of a file and got lots of weird stuff scrolling on your screen instead.

You have a million files in the same directory, and they all have similar file names. You need one specific file, but you can't remember — exactly — what you named it. You finally decide to take a wild guess and try to view the file by using the TYPE command, like this:

```
TYPE FILE.TXT
```

(Your own file name goes in place of FILE.TXT.) But after you press Enter, your screen is awash with strange characters that don't even appear on your keyboard. And the *beeping!* Somebody stop the beeping!

Antidote: Quick — press Ctrl-C.

Whew. What a relief.

Your friendly DOS prompt appears. What was the problem? You tried to view an executable file (remember those?). If the file doesn't end with TXT or DOC, you may have trouble getting a clear picture of the contents by using TYPE. The EXE files are a definite hands-off for viewing.

Whoa! That Didn't Help!

Poison: Numbers, numbers, everywhere

You pressed F9 in the DOS Shell to view the file and see five hideous columns of numbers and one column loosely resembling text.

Don't panic — that's hexadecimal, the numeric equivalent of the instructions your computer deciphers. The text out to the side is the text included in your file, although it may look strange, too.

Antidote: Press F9 again. DOS displays the file in regular text form.

Note: From the DOS Shell, you can view your file in Hex (that's the view with the columns of numbers) or in ASCII (that's straight text form).

Let's Sort This Out

Poison: Files of a feather flock together

So we've established that you've got a gazillion files stuck into this one directory, and you're having quite a time trying to find the one you need.

Do you know the extension?

Did the file end with TXT, DOC, WK1, or PNT? Was it a graphics file (BMP, WPG, PCX, TIF)? If you know the extension, you can arrange the files so you'll at least be in the right neighborhood.

Use the DIR command with a wildcard and the extension. For example, type **DIR *.BMP** to see only the BMP files.

What is this ZIP stuff?

Poison: There were supposed to be a lot of files on this disk, but there's only one and it ends in ZIP — what gives?

Antidote: You probably *do* have a disk full of stuff, even though it doesn't seem like it now. ZIP files are made with a utility called PKZIP. It squashes and packs a bunch of files into a single ZIP file. To open a ZIPped file, you need another utility called PKUNZIP (they really *did* try to make this easy). Here's how to do it:

```
PKUNZIP SMUSHED.ZIP
```

And then press Enter. This unpacks all those squashed files into your current directory.

Type **PKZIP /?** or **PKUNZIP /?** for some intimidating lists of options. For real help or copies of these utilities (because they don't come with DOS), consult your witch doctor.

Poison: PKUNZIP says the .ZIP file is damaged

Antidote: You have two ways out of this:

➦ Use your backup copy.

➦ Try to repair the ZIP file. You need a utility called PKZIPFIX. If you don't have it, call your witch doctor. Type **PKZIPFIX ITSAMESS.ZIP** and press Enter. The utility puts whatever it can salvage in a new file called PKFIXED.ZIP.

Why Doesn't My File Show Up Now?

Poison: Copied or renamed a file (document, spreadsheet, presentation, and so on), and it doesn't show up in the application

Antidote: The application is just listing the files it recognizes. Most programs look for files with certain extensions:

.WKS	Lotus 123 v1.x
.WK1	Lotus 123 v2.x
.DOC	WordPerfect and Microsoft Word (all versions)
.XLS	Microsoft Excel (all versions)
.DB	Paradox and dBASE (all versions)

When you copy or rename a file, make sure to get the extension on the new name.

You can make extensions automatic with the star (*). COPY IM_HERE.DOC HERE_TOO.* lets DOS put the extension on by itself (creating HERE_TOO.DOC). As long as the original is right, the copy will be, too.

The 99-Percent Cure for Missing Files

To sum up, here's the lowdown on file locating:

➦ First, make sure you typed the file name correctly.

➦ Next, make sure you're in the right directory.

➡ Use DIR to try to find the file.

➡ Look in the directory of the program you were using when you created the file. Check any subdirectories, too.

➡ Check the file date and time information in the DIR /S listing to see whether that gives you a clue about the file you want.

➡ Use the TYPE command to display the contents of individual files.

➡ If your application program has a special file management or document browsing option, use it.

Tips for Not Losing Files in the First Place

It's a lot easier to *not* lose files than it is to find them after you lose them. (Huh?) You'll always find

them in the last place you look. To keep better track of your files, make it a habit to do the following:

➧ Keep files in the directories they belong in.

➧ Create some file-naming rules — and stick to them.

➧ Keep backup copies of all important files.

➧ Label your disks clearly so you know what files are on what disks.

➧ Run CHKDSK /F every month or so to make sure things are still hunky-dory with your file allocation table.

DOS 6.2 Users: Use your super-duper SCANDISK command for an infinitely more thorough monthly check. Use the surface scan option every couple of months. Do it more often if you want; over-SCANDISKing doesn't hurt anything.

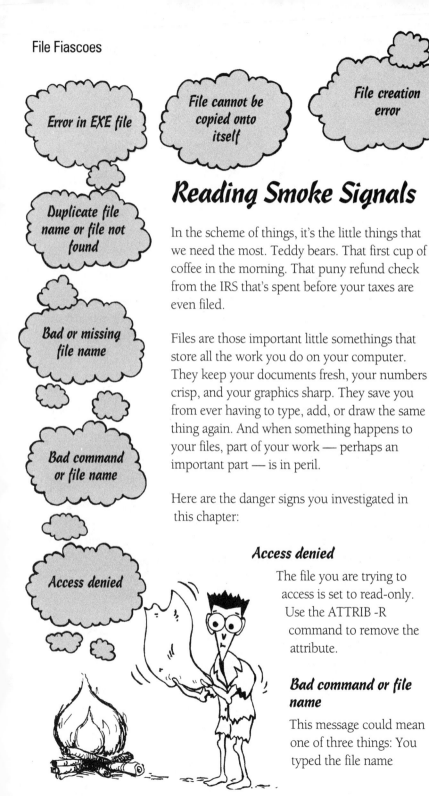

Error in EXE file

File cannot be copied onto itself

File creation error

Duplicate file name or file not found

Bad or missing file name

Bad command or file name

Access denied

Reading Smoke Signals

In the scheme of things, it's the little things that we need the most. Teddy bears. That first cup of coffee in the morning. That puny refund check from the IRS that's spent before your taxes are even filed.

Files are those important little somethings that store all the work you do on your computer. They keep your documents fresh, your numbers crisp, and your graphics sharp. They save you from ever having to type, add, or draw the same thing again. And when something happens to your files, part of your work — perhaps an important part — is in peril.

Here are the danger signs you investigated in this chapter:

Access denied

The file you are trying to access is set to read-only. Use the ATTRIB -R command to remove the attribute.

Bad command or file name

This message could mean one of three things: You typed the file name

incorrectly (oh, come on — admit it); you aren't in the right directory; or there's no such file.

Bad or missing file name

It seems logical enough to look up this error message in the chapter on files. Something is wrong with a file name, right? But this message shows up when you are first starting your machine and DOS tries to load one of the files it uses during startup. Usually the bad or missing file has something to do with instructions the computer needs in order to work with your printer, mouse, or other additional device. Because the sleuthing involved could cover a whole range of hardware items, you'll sleep better if you get the witch doctor involved right from the start.

Duplicate file name or file not found

Ah, time for an easy one. This error message covers two different situations. First, if you are renaming a file and accidentally type the same name for both the original and the new name (and how often does *that* happen?), DOS will tell you that you're duplicating an existing name. Second, you'll see this message if you mistype the original name, telling DOS it's named something it isn't. Just to be sure, be careful with your typing and read over what you've entered — especially when you're renaming files — before you press Enter.

Error in EXE file

DOS has found a — perhaps serious — hiccup in the program file you are trying to run. Write down the error message and contact your witch doctor or phone your program's technical support number as soon as possible.

File cannot be copied onto itself

This DOS remark is one of those head-thumping error messages that you hope occurs when no one is looking over your shoulder. It means that you were trying to copy a file and forgot to enter the new drive and directory for the new file. Remember that if you're giving the copy the same file name as the original, you have to put the copy in a different directory. Check your command line and try again.

File creation error

You want to create a file, and DOS won't let you. Either you're trying to give the file a name that is already in use or your disk is full and needs to be pruned. If it's not, you may have been trying to do something illegal, such as giving a file the same name as important DOS stuff.

File not found

Here's another message telling you that what DOS thinks you're looking for doesn't exist anywhere close. Check your spelling, make sure you're in the right directory, and use DIR to locate the file.

Write failure, diskette unusable

This is a nasty one. It means that the file allocation table on the disk you're using has gone bad (hopefully it's not drive C). Take the disk out (if it's a floppy) and throw it away; there's no hope for it.

Write protect error

Again, you've bitten into a write-protected disk or file. The one you're trying to use is write-protected. Remove the write-protection by removing the tab (on 5.25-inch disks) or flipping the switch (on 3.5-inch disks).

What to Tell the Witch Doctor about Your Problem

Be ready to tell the witch doctor everything you know about your symptoms as best you can (and with as little embellishment as possible):

🖐 What apparently died/what problem occurred

🖐 Any deathbed error messages it gasped before expiring

🖐 When it last worked correctly (if ever)

🖐 Any changes in the environment (office remodeling?)

🖐 The last thing you did before the crisis hit

🖐 Who touched it last

🖐 What's been done to the machine recently (new software or hardware, new network connection?)

🖐 First time, sporadic, or recurring problem?

🖐 What you've tried

🖐 What you think the problem may be

🖐 Anything else you can think of

Don't be offended if the witch doctor asks you to go back through some steps you've already tried. He's likely checking for clues so small and infinitely technical that you didn't notice them.

You Know You're Really in Trouble When . . .

You see the message File allocation table bad, drive C

This message means that DOS isn't able to read the FAT on your hard drive, which is serious business (and means serious tech-support bills). Don't take any chances and mess with the system yourself — call a reptile-wrestling miracle-worker to fix this one for you.

If it wasn't for the fog, you might have avoided the quicksand. It's a good thing that the witch doctor is there to pull you out. Maybe he's not such a bad guy afterall.

You copy files to a backup disk but can't find the disk when your work disk crashes

Yes, I've been lecturing you to make backups of your important data. Yes, that means copying the files to a disk that you put somewhere safe. In addition to being safe, that somewhere should be logical — someplace you can find easily later. In a drawer with 1,000 other diskettes is not a safe place. Inside a file folder with projects from the 1980s is not a logical place. For best results, label the disk clearly, get a disk box, and keep all important disks together.

Your office catches on fire

Some oh-so-cautious souls go to great pains to protect their data files. They carry their work home with them every night. They put backups of important contracts in safety deposit boxes. They make sure that their backups are somewhere close at all times. Seem a little silly? If you keep that important data on your desk beside your computer and — horror of horrors — there's a fire, flood, or other natural disaster, both your computer and your data are gone. If you had your data with you — or somewhere else safe — you'd have all your work. Programs are relatively easy to replace. Data can be irreplaceable.

Every computer user (myself included) should be a little paranoid about data. A firm base of paranoia makes for excellent backups. But making the backups isn't the whole song and dance — the refrain is " . . . and store them somewhere safe." Find the happy medium (her name is often Ursula — no, I do not know why) between readily available and yet not right there at your desk.

Your dog has a hankering for mylar

You've heard of cats that sleep compulsively on top of monitors? Well, dogs experience their own cravings. One dog I know likes television remote-controls and disposable cigarette lighters for dessert. If your dog is a free-thinking sort, always looking for a new taste delight, protect your disks. The soft plastic mylar of a 5.25-inch disk doesn't stand up well to any significant pressure, much less to canine molars.

Another chapter mastered! The next one takes you up to the abyss so you can stare fate — or is it format? — right in the eye.

Chapter 6   Frantic Formatting

Paths through Peril

Now we're coming up on an ominous sight: the Forest of Formats. Inside this dark, dense wood, intruders often find themselves changed into something quite different. Formatted, in other words. It is a place of many transformations.

Amazing. Curious stuff here in the forest. But wait! The natives are here and frolicking about. Some kind of crazy, ritualistic dance. You aren't sure whether to fear them or just kick back and have a good time. Still no sign of human sacrifices or voodoo dolls, but you never can tell about these things. It all seems so dangerous. Maybe it is time to move on.

Fun Format Facts

FORMAT, the subject of this chapter, is one of the most feared of all DOS commands. And for good reason. Although formatting is a necessary task (your disks must be formatted before the data will stick), it is also a dangerous one. After you type **FORMAT** and answer Y to the prompts, DOS wipes out whatever once lived on the disk.

FORMAT does have its good points. (Okay, so I'm trying to lull you into a false sense of security.) You may remember the following Important Concepts about formatting from your *DOS For Dummies* days:

- Formatting is for disks only. You can't format a single directory (nor do you need to).

- Formatting prepares the disk to store data. Both diskettes and hard disks must be formatted before you can put data on them.

- You should rarely in your lifetime have to format your hard disk. Teach your fingers to stay away from the C and D keys when you're using FORMAT.

- The FORMAT command is a little particular. You have to know the right number to put after the command itself (that number depends on the density of the disk).

- You can buy disks that are already formatted so you don't have to mess with formatting. The downside is that these disks are somewhat more expensive.

When you're suffering from strange computer maladies such as disk slowness and incessant beeping, some people who think they know but really don't may tell you that what your hard disk needs is a good format. They are referring to the process of taking all the files off the disk, reformatting the disk, and putting all the files back. In some cases, this tactic can clean things up a bit and help your computer fly right. But it is not something you decide upon lightly. If your computer symptoms are that worrisome, take your computer to the nearest MedCheck or call your tech support person for help.

Three Things You Should Always Do before You Format

1. Read the disk label.

2. Type **DIR A:** (if the disk is in drive A) or **DIR B:** (if the disk is in drive B) to make sure you don't need any of the files on the disk.

3. Look at the disk box (or label) to see whether the disk is high-density or low-density.

It Just Won't Format, Part One

The tech support person just walked away. You can still see the top of his head over the cubicle walls as he weaves toward the coffee machine.

You slide a disk into drive A, close the drive door, type **FORMAT A:**, and press Enter. And DOS says

```
Bad command or file name
```

Now how is that possible? The tech support guy just told you how to format the disk. You wrote it down.

The biggest culprit (you know the refrain by now) is that old Misplaced Finger Dance. Did you type FORMAT, FROMAT, or FOMRAT? Press F3 to find out.

Also make sure that the disk is in the drive right-side-up. (No? I won't tell.)

Where, Oh, Where Has That Little Disk Gone?

Here's another simple one.

You psyched yourself up for tackling this FORMAT thing. No little six-letter command is going to intimidate you, by golly. You put the disk in the drive — you can do that before or after you enter the command, you know — type the command, and press Enter. DOS sends you a message:

```
Invalid drive specification
```

There are only two explanations for this error. The first (cross your fingers) is that you specified a drive that doesn't exist. For example, you see this error message if you type

```
FORMAT E:
```

when you don't have a drive E.

The other possible explanation (the one you don't want) is that for some reason DOS isn't seeing the drive you want to use. Press F3 to check what you typed; if the drive you entered really is a drive, better go nab Mr. Tech Support from the coffee line.

Not Ready for What?

Disks can be stubborn little beasties. You checked your spelling and started the FORMAT command. DOS tells you to

```
Insert new diskette for drive B:
and press ENTER when ready. . .
```

The disk is in the drive, so you press Enter. And DOS says

```
Not ready
```

Not ready? For what? Hasn't DOS had its granola? Didn't it have time to read the morning paper? You've got to get to work here.

Easy — don't get too testy. You forgot to put the disk in the drive. (Or you put the disk in the wrong drive.) Check where you put the disk and which drive you told DOS to work with (press F3 to display the command you just entered).

Retype anything necessary and press Enter. Chances are, DOS will cooperate. (Although we're all a little less grumpy after we've had our granola . . .)

It Just Won't Format, Part Two

Well, we're narrowing it down, aren't we? Another obstacle you'll have to overcome (or go around) in the Forest of Format is

```
Attempted write-protect violation
```

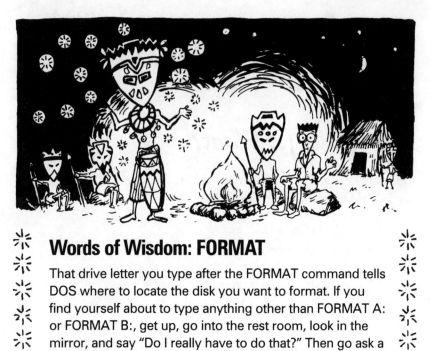

Words of Wisdom: FORMAT

That drive letter you type after the FORMAT command tells DOS where to locate the disk you want to format. If you find yourself about to type anything other than FORMAT A: or FORMAT B:, get up, go into the rest room, look in the mirror, and say "Do I really have to do that?" Then go ask a DOS-fluent person the same thing before proceeding.

Sounds pretty serious, doesn't it? Look over your shoulder, quick. Do you see any Format Cops? (They're the ones with plaid ties and plastic pocket protectors.)

Relax. All you did was try to format a write-protected disk. And that's easy to do if you're used to grabbing any old disk from the dead disks bin.

You'll know a disk is write-protected if:

➥ A little silver or black stick-on tab covers the notch on 5.25-inch disks.

➥ The switch along the bottom of a 3.5-inch disk is flipped to the opposite of where it's usually positioned.

➥ You get the `Attempted write-protect violation` error.

How to fix it? Simple. Take the disk out of the drive and flip the switch or remove the tab (don't get out the steamer — it just peels off). Then you can try to format again.

Obviously, you can format a disk that's already been formatted. Why would you do such a thing? Formatting a disk is like one level above your basic cleaning — it puts things back in order and straightens things up like new. When you erase the data on a disk, it's like using an eraser on a chalkboard. But when you format the thing, you're washing it down good.

Using the Wrong Disk in the Wrong Place at the Wrong Time

You take the greatest precautions. You carefully label all your disks. You mark them with HD or LD (for high- and low-density). You explain your

**Work-Every-Time Excuses:
"I Did That Intentionally."**

You have to be a really good actor to pull this one off. We all screw up — some worse than others. But to make other people think what we did was intentional — now that's art.

Tech support person: Do you know you have 15 copies of the file NEWDOC.DOC?

You: I did that intentionally.

Boss: Do you know that you spent over 50 hours on-line to Tahiti Tourism?

You: I did that intentionally.

IRS: Do you know you overpaid $5,000 on last year's tax returns?

You: Really?

organizational scheme to all your officemates so that just in case they decide to go messing around with your stuff, at least they won't move your disks around.

But one day, when The Boss is looking over your shoulder, you grab a disk, slide it in the slot, type **FORMAT**, and see

```
Disk unusable
```

"What's that?" asks The Boss, looking closer.

Heh-heh. Wrong disk, you mumble, scrambling to find a disk you know will work.

After a little shuffling, you find one of those high-density disks you marked so carefully. You put it in the drive, type the necessary command, and formatting begins.

The Fab Four FORMATs

DOS provides you with four FORMAT command options. Well, actually, you do have other options, but they involve drives C and D, which you already know you shouldn't touch.

You really want to see all four options in black and white, don't you? Okay, here they are:

FORMAT A: Formats the disk in drive A to match the density of the drive (low for low-density; high for high-density).

FORMAT B: Formats the disk in drive B to match the density of the drive (same refrain).

FORMAT A:/F:360   Formats the 5.25-inch disk in drive A to low-density format (even though the drive is a high-density drive).

FORMAT B:/F:720   Formats the 3.5-inch disk in drive B to low-density format (even though the drive is a high-density drive).

Now that we've straightened that mess out, let's move on to la grande dame of all FORMAT faux pas.

I Formatted the Wrong Disk!

Poison: The FORMAT of no return

You had a disk full of files in drive A. You wanted to make a copy of it on the disk in drive B. Just as you were ready to make the copy, you remembered that the disk in drive B hasn't been formatted. So you type

```
FORMAT A:
```

and follow the prompts on the screen. The disk light on drive A comes on, as DOS starts wiping away all your data.

Hey — wait a minute. Drive A? Didn't you mean to format the disk in drive B? Quick! What key do I push?

Well, you can try pressing Esc or Ctrl-C, but nothing is going to work. Let it run its course and learn your lesson: Use FORMAT with caution.

So you're sitting at your computer and your head is starting to throb. How many files did you lose? How long will it take you to recover or reenter them? *Can* you reenter them?

Words of Wisdom: MSD

If you've got all the manuals that came with your system, you can look up the information. (Oh sure, we all keep the manuals. But where did we put them?) Or you can type

```
MSD
```

at the DOS prompt and press Enter. The opening screen of Microsoft Diagnostics appears and flashes a message saying that the utility is looking at your system. (Don't blush.)

The Microsoft Diagnostics program is available with DOS 5.0 and later versions.

Another screen appears, showing you various information about your computer. You can see what CPU you've got, how much memory you have, and a lot of other things you shouldn't particularly care about. At the top of the column on the right side of the screen, however, you see

```
Disk Drives . . .
```

Press D. Another screen appears, this one telling you information about your disk drives (which includes both hard drives and diskette drives). You're interested in the line beside the A: and B:. If it says

```
Floppy Drive, 5.25" 1.2MB
```

you've got a high-density drive. Here's how the different types shake out:

```
Floppy Drive, 5.25" 1.2MB       High-density
Floppy Drive, 5.25" 360K        Low-density
Floppy Drive, 3.5" 1.44MB       High-density
Floppy Drive, 3.5" 720K         Low-density
```

When you're finished poking around in MSD — go ahead, poke away; you can't hurt anything — press F3 to exit the program.

Antidote: Boy, are you lucky. Just a couple of years ago, I would have looked sympathetically out from the pages of this book, shook my head, and said, "Sorry. Can't help you."

But today, in this age of not-computer-literate-but-faking-it users, there is a safety net to catch us. Thank heavens.

The safety net is called UNFORMAT. You've got it if you have DOS 5.0 or later.

At the DOS prompt, type **UNFORMAT.** The hard disk clunks a minute, and then a screen appears telling you that Unformat can recover an accidentally formatted hard disk (ouch!) or diskette and can retrieve virus-blown or electrically spiked files. You might not recover all your files this way, but it's a lot better than losing everything.

Follow the yellow-brick prompts through the process. (But don't rest in the Field of Poppies — they're drugged.)

When you're all through, go get some M&Ms — oops, I forgot we're on an island, better make it a coconut — and take a rest.

We've met the enemy, and they is us.

Lowering Disk Expectations

Every disk I've ever met longs to be a system disk. Oh, sure, all disks can store data. They all can hold files. But only important disks can start programs. And only those omnipotent system disks can actually start the operating system on your computer.

Oh, to be a system disk.

It's easy for us humans to make our disks into system disks. You learned how in Chapter 1. Remember? You use the FORMAT command with /S to add the necessary system files. And then voilà! Your disk is capable of starting your computer, even when your hard disk can't. (You have to admit, that's a pretty important role.)

But what happens when you type **FORMAT /S** and DOS says

```
Disk unsuitable for system disk
```

Well, first of all, you're going to have a very disappointed disk. DOS found some bad spots on the disk right where it needs to put the system files.

You can try using CHKDSK to sleuth out the problem, but the disk's aspirations are probably over for good. You can still use the disk to store ordinary data, though, as long as you keep an eye on those bad sectors. (CHKDSK will be glad to help you do that.)

A Bad Sector Haiku

Little black square thing
Holding all my data files
Why'd you go so wrong?

Well, you have to have the right attitude to understand the poetry. And when you're dealing with bad sectors at the worst possible moment, you may not be capable of seeing the beauty in things.

If there is beauty to see.

So you're still trying to format that blasted disk, huh? And this time, DOS says

```
Unable to write BOOT
```

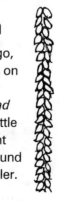

Techie Term

In computer lingo, those bad spots on your disk are referred to as *bad sectors.* Just a little jargon you might want to toss around at the water cooler.

This is another dead-in-the-water problem. Don't do anything with that disk except throw it in the general direction of your trash can. Don't try to talk DOS out of such a stern message. Go along quietly. Get another disk.

Mutant Disks from Hell

Here's another one of those can't-get-no-satisfaction errors:

```
Invalid media or Track 0 bad — disk unusable
```

Work-Every-Time Excuses: "My Cat Did It."

This is an adult variation of the old cat-ate-my-homework bit. It actually does work sometimes. It is possible for a cat to walk across the keyboard in such a way that is spells FORMAT. Even FORMAT A or C is possible. The colon, however, is another thing. How did you get your cat to press and hold the Shift key while typing the colon? Your odds are even further decreased when you're trying to blame the cat for accidental COPYs.

But here's an alternative:

"I was getting ready to copy a bunch of files when I realized that it would mess up some things on my hard disk. I was just getting ready to erase the mistake, when that blasted cat jumped down from the monitor and landed on the Enter key."

Oh bad, bad kitty.

You may as well face it: There's no using this particular disk. Toss it out and get another. If DOS sends you this message a lot (when you're working with different disks, of course), you may need to find a better place to keep your extra disks. Are they in a box, somewhere safe? Or are they thrown in a pile, in the dark bottom of a forgotten desk drawer? Are they sitting in the windowsill, enjoying the 95-degree August heat?

Disk-A-Mania

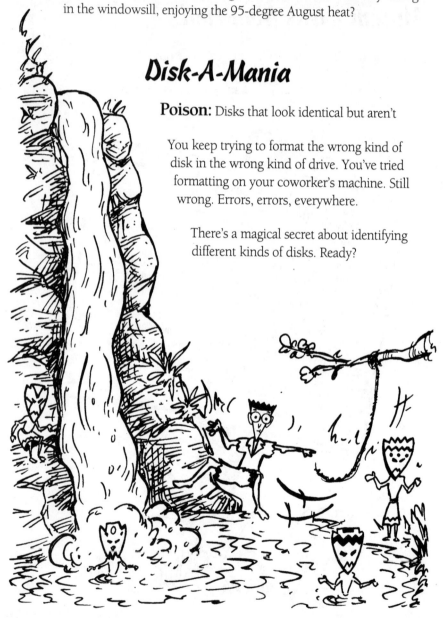

Poison: Disks that look identical but aren't

You keep trying to format the wrong kind of disk in the wrong kind of drive. You've tried formatting on your coworker's machine. Still wrong. Errors, errors, everywhere.

There's a magical secret about identifying different kinds of disks. Ready?

Antidote: The way you tell which disk is what kind depends on the type of disk you're using:

- If you're using a 5.25-inch disk, a low-density disk has an extra ring around the hole in the center of the disk (it's called the hub ring). A high-density disk is just bare mylar around the center hole.

- If you're using a 3.5-inch disk, a high-density disk will have an extra hole in the lower right corner. It's lower capacity cousin is lacking the hole.

FDISK File Fatalities

Poison: FDISK peer pressure

You're getting a couple of weird errors, and someone told you to use FDISK.

Antidote: *Don't.* FDISK doesn't have anything to do with formatting diskettes; it's the utility you use to format a hard drive and set up partitions.

Never, ever attempt to do any toying with FDISK. Only qualified personnel — witch doctors — understand the subtle atrocities and invisible hazards that could befall you.

Last-Minute Labeling

Poison: Overlooked volume labels

You just formatted a disk and forgot to add a volume label. Now you're kicking yourself.

Antidote: Use the LABEL command to add a volume label. Just type LABEL, followed by a space, the drive, a colon, and the label you want to add (up to eleven characters, no spaces). For example, the following line names the disk in drive A FROGLEGS:

```
LABEL A:FROGLEGS
```

Now why you'd want to name a disk FROGLEGS or how it might help you in the future is a little unclear, but, hey — whatever works, right?

The Long, Boring FORMAT

Poison: Fall-asleep formatting

So it's fallen to you to format this incredible stack of already-used disks everyone in your department has dropped on your desk. Lucky you — you get to reformat them. Why is it your job? Because you've finished everything else, of course.

If the disks you're formatting will not be holding extremely important data — that is, the data will be stored in at least two other locations in addition to the disk — you could do a quick format, get the task over with, and head for home a little early.

Antidote: QuickFormat is a little switch DOS lets you get by with when you're dog-tired of doing the long version. To tell DOS to QuickFormat a disk, put the disk in the drive and type

```
FORMAT A: /Q
```

If you've got a disk in drive B, of course, type

```
FORMAT B: /Q
```

Same thing, different drive.

Techie Term

Reformatting is the process of erasing all data on the disk and preparing it to store more data — like new.

What's the Best Way to Interact With the Witch Doctor?

As a being that's exposed to another realm, the witch doctor may be used to speaking a different language. Here are some tips for easing communication with your witch doctor:

- Describe the problem factually

- Listen carefully

- If you don't understand what's being said, ask for clarification

- Take notes of things the witch doctor tries

- Don't walk away — he may need to ask questions

- Let him know how important or unimportant this is

- Try to stay out of the way

- Do what the witch doctor says *when* he says it — don't go off on tangents of your own

- Remember that a little Thanks goes a long way

If you're going to be storing really important stuff on the disk, use the traditional FORMAT. Keeping your files safe is worth the few-minutes' wait.

No-Go Formats

Poison: A disk that won't format

You're trying to reformat a disk you've used before. The disk is a acting little strange — it's been giving you miscellaneous errors for the last few days.

Antidote: First, copy any files off that disk that are important. Then, with the disk in the drive (drive A, for example), type

```
FORMAT A: /U
```

This tells DOS to unconditionally format the disk. No matter what. DOS will force the disk to take the format (unless the disk is really trashed).

Even though the disk is usable once the format has been done, remember that the disk — in its past life — was a little shaky on the integrity meter. Don't keep anything too important on that disk. And always keep a backup.

A Few Error Messages We'd Like to See
- It's time to clean off that hard disk.
- Did you make a backup?
- Bill Gates says "Hi!"
- My, you look nice today.
- The report you did was great.
- Fresh coffee in the break room!
- Illegal weekend use. Go home. Take a break!

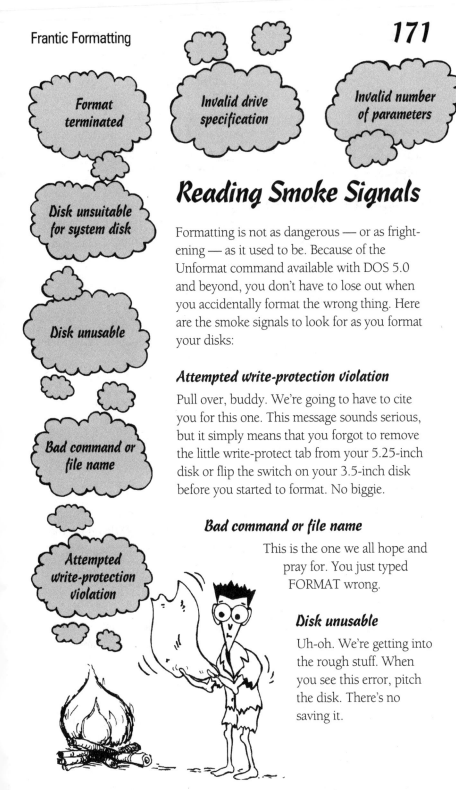

Format terminated

Invalid drive specification

Invalid number of parameters

Disk unsuitable for system disk

Disk unusable

Bad command or file name

Attempted write-protection violation

Reading Smoke Signals

Formatting is not as dangerous — or as frightening — as it used to be. Because of the Unformat command available with DOS 5.0 and beyond, you don't have to lose out when you accidentally format the wrong thing. Here are the smoke signals to look for as you format your disks:

Attempted write-protection violation

Pull over, buddy. We're going to have to cite you for this one. This message sounds serious, but it simply means that you forgot to remove the little write-protect tab from your 5.25-inch disk or flip the switch on your 3.5-inch disk before you started to format. No biggie.

Bad command or file name

This is the one we all hope and pray for. You just typed FORMAT wrong.

Disk unusable

Uh-oh. We're getting into the rough stuff. When you see this error, pitch the disk. There's no saving it.

Disk unsuitable for system disk

When DOS tried to put the all-important system files on your disk (in order to create a boot disk), it found bad spots in crucial places. Just to be safe, pitch the disk and get another one.

Format terminated. Format another (Y/N)?

No offense, but DOS *really* doesn't like that disk you're trying to format.The disk could be bad, as in defective, or you could be trying to use the wrong density disk in the wrong type of drive.

Invalid drive specification

DOS isn't seeing the drive you specified in your command line. Make sure that you specified the right drive (it should be something like A:, B:, C:, or D: — and don't forget the colon). Then try again.

Invalid number of parameters

Take a look at that FORMAT command line you just typed. Did you type too many drive names? Did you enter a path by mistake? Did you get the density right? If you're not sure, press F3 to display what you entered. Make any necessary modifications and try again.

Not ready

Something is not the way it should be, but at least it's something simple. Check to make sure that the disk is in the drive you think it's in and that the disk drive is closed.

Unable to write BOOT

This is one of those it's-all-over-Uncle-Charley messages. Get rid of the disk.

You Know You're Really in Trouble When . . .

One after one, your disks are all bad

If you keep seeing FORMAT errors over and over, first consider where you keep your disks. Could they be getting damaged? If not, could they be victims of virus warfare? If more than two of your disks refuse to format, something bigger may be going on. Call someone wiser to help you decipher the problem.

You have one hundred diskettes with no labels and you need to take a clean, newly formatted disk to a meeting in two minutes

Tsk, tsk, tsk. What did I tell you? Label those disks! Then you can avoid the guesswork (at least if you keep the labels current). You won't find yourself crossing your fingers and hoping that there wasn't anything important on the disk you just formatted.

You keep seeing Invalid drive specification even though the drive is valid

DOS isn't recognizing the drive you want it to use, so you have some kind of hardware problem. A cable may be disconnected, or some other monstrous hex may be controlling your machine. Find someone with experience to figure this one out.

You're working at someone else's machine and, not being sure which drive is which, you type FORMAT C:

If you haven't pressed Enter yet, don't! If you pressed Enter but haven't done anything else, you can back out of the process by typing **N** when DOS asks Are you sure? But if you went ahead and blindly reformatted the hard disk, hang your head and go confess to someone who can bail you out. Don't attempt to use UNFORMAT on a hard disk by yourself (especially without knowing what was on the hard disk in the first place).

You get an Invalid media or Track 0 bad error on your hard disk

Time for that HoneyBun you've been thinking about. Get as far away from your computer as possible — go over and visit the people in the art department for a while. When you're able to face it, come back to your office but bring someone else with you. Your hard disk has turned on you, and things are going to get ugly. This error message often occurs when there's been some physical damage to the disk. Like all the other dead-in-the-drive error messages, it means that you need to use a disk other than this one.

Chapter 7

Cryptic Commands

Paths through Peril

Command Caverns is a series of dark and musty caves carved deep into the mountainside by years of tropical floods. Be careful because creepy crawly things abound in here — things with eight legs (ugh!), four legs (yikes!), two wings (duck!), and, the worst of all horrors, DOS commands.

When Commands Act Weird, Try These Things First

There's something to be said for the process of elimination. If your cookies turn out runny, you check the amount of sugar in the recipe. If your sugar measurement was correct, you double-check the oven temperature. If that's not the problem, you check to see whether you made a mistake with the flour. By carefully retracing your steps, you can usually discover where you took a wrong turn.

If your car is leaking oil, you look . . . uh . . . somewhere under the hood. And then you call the witch doctor.

Hmmm. Looks like a cavern ahead. And a passageway that probably leads to somewhere. Can't quite make out the writing on the wall. Some form of hieroglyphics or something. You wonder what does it all mean? Where does it all lead to?

If your commands are misbehaving, make sure that these things aren't the cause:

🔹 **Did you type the command correctly?** Watch that spelling.

🔹 *Is there such a command?* DOS cooperates only if you enter a command that it recognizes — and the command must be available in the version of DOS that you use. If you try to use the UNDELETE command with DOS 4.0, for example, you get a "Huh?" message.

🔹 **Did you enter the path name correctly?** If you have to tell DOS where to find a certain file and you botch it up, DOS wanders away in the wrong direction and eventually comes back to you with a big zero.

🔹 **Did you include all parts of the command?** Some commands, such as the ever-popular COPY, require that you tell DOS where to copy from and where to copy to. If you forget one or the other, you get bit.

Don't Forget to Ask for Help

Unless you have magical powers, you'll need to do a little research the first time you use a DOS command. You can look in a good book, or you can use DOS's built-in help system to get the feel of things.

Suppose that you're having trouble with the COPY command. You can get help by typing

```
HELP COPY
```

and pressing Enter. A lot of information appears, with the first line explaining what you can do with the command.

To display a listing of all DOS commands and their one-line definitions, just type **HELP** and press Enter. Seven screenfuls of information appear, one at a time. If you're not sure how to use help, type **HELP HELP** and press Enter. But don't be surprised if someone from security runs over, thinking that you're in some kind of danger.

How to Enter Commands the Wrong Way

Until you start trying to use DOS commands, you don't realize how many wrong ways there are to enter them. Most people make the following mistakes (at least a few times):

- They forget to put a backslash between directory names. For example, they enter

    `C:WORD SOS` rather than `C:\WORD\SOS`

- They accidentally add extra spaces in the command line, like this:

    `RENAME A: PARTRIDG PEARTREE`

- They forget what directory they're in.

- They use the wildcards * and ? incorrectly and get unexpected results.

- They enter incomplete file names. For example, they type

    `MYFILE` rather than `MYFILE.DOC`

For help with entering DOS commands, consult *DOS For Dummies* on the bewitching and bewildering topic of *syntax*.

Directory Moves and Misnomers?

Poison: Badly named directories

Everybody makes fun of your directory names, and you're tired of it. So what if you named your directories FRED, WILMA, BARNEY, and BETTY? You know what's in them.

But you're tired of taking the heat, and you want to rename the directories. What's the command for renaming directories? REN won't work.

Antidote: Use MOVE to change the name of the directory. The directory will have to stay in the same place, but FRED can become anything you want it to with a simple command line:

```
MOVE C:\FRED C:\NEWDIR
```

There. Now you're more conventional. (But what would Dino say?)

DISKCOPY Doesn't

COPY is great when you're copying individual files or groups of files. If you want to copy an entire disk, however, DISKCOPY is a lot easier to use (and not quite as sneaky).

Oh, but I didn't say it was perfect, did I? DISKCOPY, as good-natured as it is, can still bring you face-to-face with a problem you didn't expect: incompatible disk sizes.

DISKCOPY copies a disk track by track to another disk. When it's finished, you have an exact duplicate of the original disk. (That's why people use this command to make backups.)

If you try to copy a high-density disk onto a low-density disk, what's going to happen? Right. All the data won't fit. DOS will prompt you to insert another disk to hold the leftover data. But it's a lot cleaner to just start out with a disk that's the same density as the one you want to copy.

Poison: Copy refusals

You were following instructions and tried to use DISKCOPY to make a backup copy of a program disk. You stuck the original program disk in drive A, put another disk in drive B, and entered the DISKCOPY command:

```
DISKCOPY A: B:
```

It should work, right? But right after DOS starts reading the disk, it stops short and says very politely

```
Copy process ended
Copy another diskette (Y/N)?
```

No, you want to copy *this* diskette. What does DOS want from you?

Antidote: DISKCOPY is one of those *particular* commands. Everything has to be just so. DISKCOPY will refuse to work if the disks you've got in those drives are different. For example, if you've got a 5.25-inch high-density floppy in drive A (that's 1.2MB) and a 3.5-inch high-density disk in drive B (that's 1.44MB), DISKCOPY will cheerfully deliver that error message.

To get around DISKCOPY's hangups, copy the disk in drive A to another disk you put in drive A. (Or, better

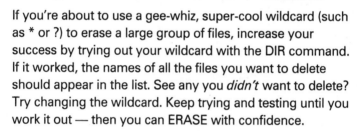

Words of Wisdom: DIR to Test Wildcards

If you're about to use a gee-whiz, super-cool wildcard (such as * or ?) to erase a large group of files, increase your success by trying out your wildcard with the DIR command. If it worked, the names of all the files you want to delete should appear in the list. See any you *didn't* want to delete? Try changing the wildcard. Keep trying and testing until you work it out — then you can ERASE with confidence.

yet, use XCOPY instead.) DOS will tell you when to swap the floppies. Here's the command line:

```
DISKCOPY A: A:
```

When you use the DISKCOPY command with DOS version 6.2, DOS will use your hard disk to store the files temporarily before copying them over to the second disk. As a result, the DISKCOPY is lots faster.

ERASE-ing Erratically

You did it, didn't you? You got carried away cleaning off your hard disk and blew away those report files you need for next Friday's meeting. Hey, life's short. Why stew? DOS includes a Thank-You-Microsoft! command specifically for retrieving those files you sent to the edge of nonexistence.

Okay, play the fanfare music. Introducing

```
UNDELETE
```

You need to remember one big rule about using UNDELETE: Try to catch your mistake as quickly as possible. If you realize that you deleted 30 files you need, don't go ahead and do other work before you use UNDELETE to save the files you purged. If you do, you run the risk of writing over the space on the disk that the deleted files occupied. And if that happens, you'll never get those files back.

If you accidentally wipe out a whole directory, you can try to get all the files back in one fell swoop (or is that swell foop?) by typing

```
UNDELETE *.* /ALL
```

MOVEing Mindlessly

Poison: Long-distance moving problems

You want to move files from a directory on drive C to a directory on drive D.

Antidote: Don't try using the MOVE command. It won't cooperate. You can't actually move a directory to a different position in the scheme of things. For example, you can't use MOVE to put the

```
C:\WORD6\DATA\DEC93
```

subdirectory over here:

```
D:\PROJECTS\DEC93
```

If that's really what you want to do, copy all the files from C:\WORD6\DATA\DEC93 (use *.*) to D:\PROJECTS\DEC93 and then delete the files you don't need.

RECOVER — Don't let it even try!

Poison: Someone told you that the best way to get a lost file back was with the RECOVER command.

Antidote: If you care about your computer, ignore this advice.

Warning: Under *no circumstances* should you use the DOS RECOVER command. It will hopelessly ruin your disk, all in the name of saving a file. If the file was *that* important to start with, it's worth a call to the Witch Doctor for recovery.

In their infinite wisdom, Microsoft removed RECOVER from DOS 6.

RENAMEs Refused

Poison: What? DOS won't let you rename a file?

Antidote: Have you been swearing at DOS again? First, apologize. Then take a look at your command line (press F3 to display it). Did it look something like this:

```
REN C:\THISNAME THATNAME
```

You can call RENAME REN if you like, but it doesn't respond well to RENAPE, REMANE, or RENAIM. Watch your spelling.

RENAME also won't jump across directory lines. You renamed the file in one directory, and by golly, RENAME is going to keep it there. If you try to specify a new directory for the renamed file, RENAME tells you

```
Invalid parameter
```

This message simply means that you tried to do something that you can't do. Keep the renamed file in the same directory as the original. And remember to specify the path if the file you want to rename is in a directory other than the current one.

REPLACE Replicating

Poison: You've got a directory full of files and want to update your backup diskette. Using COPY takes forever, since it copies every file in the directory — even when they're overwriting identical files on the disk.

Antidote: Try the REPLACE command. It keeps two directories (or a hard drive subdirectory and a diskette) in synch with each other.

Here's how it's done:

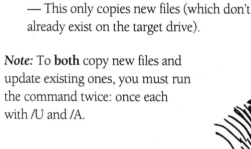 REPLACE /U C:\DOCUMENT\SOS_DOS*.* A:\ — This updates (/U) the files in drive A (A:\) with any newer files in C:\DOCUMENT\SOS_DOS. If you created a new file on drive C:, it *won't* be copied.

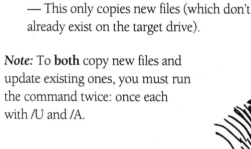 REPLACE /A C:\DOCUMENT\SOS_DOS*.* A:\ — This only copies new files (which don't already exist on the target drive).

Note: To **both** copy new files and update existing ones, you must run the command twice: once each with /U and /A.

The Path Less Raveled

Poison: Path irritation

You're sick and tired of everyone asking you whether you've entered the path right. When your computer beeps, when you can't find the right file, when your document won't print, when *anything* happens, someone asks you

whether you've got the right path to your file.

What the heck is a path and is it really *that* important?

The path tells DOS or any other program you're using where to find the file you want to work with. The path includes the drive, directory, and perhaps subdirectory where the file is located. Here's an example of a path:

```
C:\WORD6\SOSDOS7.DOC
```

This path tells DOS (or any other program) to find the SOSDOS7.DOC file on drive C in the WORD6 subdirectory. If you're trying to copy SOSDOS7.DOC to another directory and you get the path wrong (for example, if you enter C:\123\SOSDOS7.DOC), DOS looks in the 123 subdirectory for the file you want, and when it isn't found, DOS screams "Error!"

Antidote: Remember these path basics:

- The path always begins with the root of every disk (whether that disk is A, B, C, D, or whatever).
- The backslash (\) is used to show the root. For example, the root of drive C is C:\.
- After the root, the path includes the directories DOS must go through to get to the file you want.
- You can include many directories in a path, but each directory must be separated by a backslash (\).
- The last item in the path is the name of the file you're looking for. Don't include a backslash after the file name.

Make It STOP!

Poison: An accidental command that will go on forever

You're finding out all about how to enter DOS commands. You figure out which ones you'll need, how to enter paths, how to avoid COPY headaches, and all sorts of things.

But what happens when you enter a command you didn't mean to?

In some cases, your goose is cooked. If you accidentally copy a file from here to there, too late — that file is copied. If you rename a bunch of files in the wrong directory, oops — nothing you can do about it.

But if you start a DOS command that's going to go on for a while — such as copying an entire directory or displaying the contents of every directory on your hard disk — you can use a magic key combination to halt the operation midstream.

Antidote: Press Ctrl-C. That's right. Just Ctrl and C pressed at roughly the same time (or maybe Ctrl just a millisecond sooner). DOS stops whatever it was doing, displays

^C

and returns you to the DOS prompt.

Print Screen, Please

Poison: Need a printed copy of what's on the screen

All you want to do is print what's on your screen — quick. You keep getting this weird error, and whenever you tell the witch doctor about it, she says "There's no such thing." Now, if you could just get the printer to print, you could show her.

Antidote: Make sure the printer is connected to your computer and is turned on and ready. Then press your Prt Sc key. (It may say Print Screen, depending on your keyboard.) The

Techie Term

LPT1 vs. PRN? This isn't much of a fight, because the contestants are the same. LPT1 is the name of the first parallel interface (or port). PRN is DOS's default printer device, which is usually LPT1. So many terms, so much confusion. . . .

screen before you — strange message and all — should print on your printer.

After you do a quick print of your screen using Prt Sc, advance the paper by pressing your printer's form feed button. Prt Sc just dumps the text from the screen to the printer and doesn't stop to think about cleaning up its own mess.

Print Fly-by Messages, Please

Poison: Need a print-out of the messages that are flying by on your screen.

You're trying to load a program, and each time you attempt it, DOS flashes some quick message — too fast for you to read — and locks up. How can you slow things down so you can see what the trouble is?

Well, you can't. (Unless you have a finely tuned sense of timing and can press the Pause key at just the right moment.) But there's something else you can try.

Antidote: Press Ctrl-P to turn on DOS's printing feature. This acts like an on/off switch. When you press Ctrl-P, your printer begins to type everything displayed on your screen. When you press Ctrl-P again, the printing stops.

PRINT Plunders

PRINT is one of the most underrated DOS commands. It's not the source of major DOS headaches; in fact, not much can go wrong when you use it. PRINT can even help you narrow down the field of choices when you're trying to figure out what's wrong with your printer *this* time.

Suppose that you decide to print something from DOS. You type PRINT AUTOEXEC.BAT and press Enter. DOS shoots those data bits a million miles an hour out the printer port, and your printer pounds out the contents of AUTOEXEC.BAT faster than you can say "What's that?"

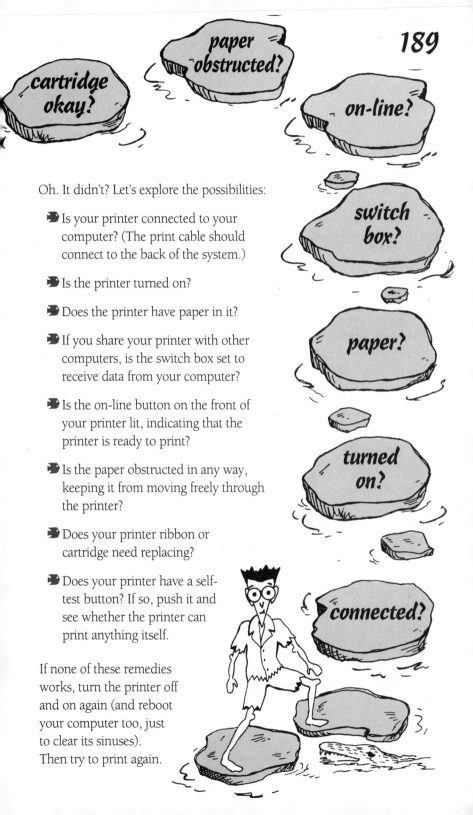

cartridge okay?

paper obstructed?

on-line?

switch box?

paper?

turned on?

connected?

Oh. It didn't? Let's explore the possibilities:

🖙 Is your printer connected to your computer? (The print cable should connect to the back of the system.)

🖙 Is the printer turned on?

🖙 Does the printer have paper in it?

🖙 If you share your printer with other computers, is the switch box set to receive data from your computer?

🖙 Is the on-line button on the front of your printer lit, indicating that the printer is ready to print?

🖙 Is the paper obstructed in any way, keeping it from moving freely through the printer?

🖙 Does your printer ribbon or cartridge need replacing?

🖙 Does your printer have a self-test button? If so, push it and see whether the printer can print anything itself.

If none of these remedies works, turn the printer off and on again (and reboot your computer too, just to clear its sinuses). Then try to print again.

If your printer continues to hold out on you, you probably have a polter-geist in your hardware or cable. Have someone with some printer-taming experience handle it for you.

1001 Ways to Print from DOS

Poison: During troubleshooting (and sometimes just for the heck of it), you want to print directly from DOS.

Antidote: DOS doesn't really give you 1001 ways to print, but it does give you three:

🖝 If you're printing a text file to LPT1, use EDIT's File/Print option. It even lets you highlight and print a portion of a file. However, you can print *only* to LPT1.

🖝 A second way to print is to use the command

```
COPY file.ext LPT1
```

If you don't want to print to LPT1, you can substitute LPT2, PRN, COM1, or whatever.

🖝 The third option is to use the DOS PRINT command. **Warning:** The PRINT command is a TSR (terminate-and-stay-resident) utility. Be careful when you use it! If you shell out of an application to do something in DOS, don't use PRINT.

Printing a Directory from DOS

Poison: You can't figure out how to print a copy of a directory listing.

Antidote: All you need to do is learn a pretty simple trick of the DOS masters. Use *redirection* to send your directory list to the printer.

First, use CD to get to the directory for which you want a directory list. Then type **DIR > LPT1** (or whatever port your printer is on). The > symbol tells DOS to take the command on the left (in this case, DIR) — which it would normally send to the screen — and send that command to the location on the right (in this case, LTP1).

In the unlikely event that you want to put a copy of a directory into a file, just put a filename after the > symbol. For example, the command

```
DIR > MY_STUFF.DIR
```

creates a file called MY_STUFF.DIR and then dumps the output of the DIR command into the file. Is that slick or what?

Words of Wisdom: Confirmation

New in DOS 6.2:

1) The MOVE, COPY, and XCOPY commands now ask you for confirmation before copying a file over another file that has the same name. (However, when issued from a batch file, these commands do not prompt for confirmation before overwriting a file.)

2) The output of the DIR, MEM, CHKDSK, and FORMAT commands is much easier to read since it now includes thousands separators when displaying numbers greater than 999. For example, "1000000 bytes free" now reads "1,000,000 bytes free."

3) The DISKCOPY command now uses your hard disk as an interim storage area, which makes copying from one floppy disk to another faster and easier.

No Response from Network Printer

Poison: You're attached to the all-mighty network, but you *still* can't take advantage of those $4,000 super-high resolution laser printers.

Antidote: The answer here is obvious, but it's kind of embarassing, so lean in close: Are you logged on to the network?

Traditionally speaking, if other people are still using the network, the network's still working. The problem has to be either with your computer, your software, or the wire from your PC to the wall. Try the following:

➧ Check the printer settings in the program.

➧ Restart the computer and log on again.

➧ Make sure that all cables are plugged in.

If all else fails, remember the cry of Those Who Would Compute: "Hey, Witch Doctor!"

The PRINT Command Doesn't Work

Poison: When you try printing from DOS with the PRINT command, your computer just locks up.

Antidote: Make sure that you're correctly answering PRINT's only question: Where is your printer attached?

If you miss this question, the quiz is over. PRINT gleefully tries to send your file to the port you indicated. In fact, it keeps trying for a long time — "a long time" being something between minutes and, well, forever.

If you have port right and you still can't get PRINT to work, try one of the other methods of printing discussed earlier in this chapter. If one of those methods works, the problem is your PRINT utility. Replace it from your master disks or from a computer that's *identical* to yours.

What's the Best Way to Avoid Bad Witch Doctor Advice?

Some well-meaning witch-doctor-wanna-bes can offer some pretty suspect advice at times. If you hear some of the following suggestions, you may want to get a second opinion before proceeding:

➤ "Your just going to have to reformat your hard drive." (This may be true, but rarely.)

➤ "Sorry, Bud, your data's gone forever." (Maybe you can use UNFORMAT or UNDELETE?)

➤ "If you don't know what those files are, just delete them." (They may be network drivers — don't touch.)

➤ "Oh, go ahead and turn your machine on and off a few times." (Sometimes this is your only choice. Other times it means you just lost your only chance to save your data.)

➤ "Hit Ctrl-Alt-Delete or Ctrl-Break — that'll do it." (Yeah, sure. And it may send pieces of your file floating into hyperspace. You should do this only when it's a last resort.) The best witch doctors are the ones who aren't out to impress you, and even the very best ones know when to say, "I'm sorry, I just don't know."

If none of the printing methods work, have the Witch Doctor check out your printer port — something's screwy there.

It's Printing, But Not in MY Language

Poison: You're working in a DOS application, and your printer adopts Gobbeltygook as its native tongue. Visions of a nice afternoon are carried away on the backs of squiggly little letters and other weird characters.

Antidote: You're dealing with a printer problem, right? Maybe, maybe not. What you definitely have is a *problem printing*. To solve it, take the following steps.

1. **Before you begin troubleshooting, always save what you're doing.** So, save your document now.

2. **Take a look at the trashed printout.** Are you doing anything "strange" in this document? Did *any* text print correctly or is the whole printout a mess?

   If your document printed just fine up to the point at which you inserted that graphic or that cute face you made out of punctuation marks, you're already on your way to a solution. Try removing the graphic. If the document prints just fine, try putting the graphic back. Garbage again? If so, you've found the culprit.

   Don't try to print anything except text files from DOS. DOS won't be able to communicate graphic images to your printer the way it needs to. For best results, print from the application you used to create the file in the first place.

3. **Did any error messages appear on-screen?** If so, the follow them up. Your word processor's manual may help translate the more esoteric ones. If you didn't get any messages, your word processor thinks that everything's just fine. (Silly program.)

4. **Check the program's printer configuration.** Is the printer listed the one that's really on your desk? Individual printers have their own unique languages (no sense having one universal language for something as trivial as printing). What are vital operating instructions for one printer will look like toddler-talk to another.

   Because you managed to get *something* out of your printer, the port assignment (LPT1, COM2, and so on) is probably correct. If nothing came out of the printer, you would need to check the program's configuration and make sure that your printer is really attached to the port the program thinks it is.

5. **Next, try printing directly from DOS.** An easy test is to type **COPY CONFIG.SYS LPT1** at the root directory of your hard disk. (The example assumes that your printer is on the first parallel port — if it's somewhere else, substitute the appropriate port for LPT1 in the command line.)

   If your printer connection is good, the contents of the CONFIG.SYS file should pour out of your printer. You then know to point the finger of blame at the program rather than at the printer or cable. Try reloading the driver software for your printer — see the program's manual for more information.

   If the printout of the CONFIG.SYS file is trashed just like the document printout, the problem is with the printer port, cable, or the printer itself. Try a different port, if you have another one. Okay, you worked your way down to the printer port. Ah, the thrill of the chase.

6. **Now check the cable.** Are the ends screwed in tightly at both the computer and printer? Is there some slack in the cable, or is it stretched tightly between your machine and the printer?

   A loose plug or a tightrope-like cable can create a less-than-optimal connection to the computer. Make sure that the plug is screwed into the port. Move the printer closer to the computer if the cable between the two is stretched too tightly.

Also check out the cable's physical appearance. Is there any furniture crimping its style? Does it have any curly-Q kinks? Printer cables are notorious for developing bad wires, particularly if they're pinned to the carpet by some furniture. If you have any reason to think that your cable may be damaged, try another one. In fact, it's probably a good idea to keep a spare cable around the office for just such occasions.

7. **You've arrived at the printer; is it set up properly?** Are the printer settings correct? Check the "Print Plunders" section in this chapter for further assistance. Run the printer's self-test (check the manual for specific instructions). If it fails, you really *do* have a printer problem. If the printer passes the self-test, however, you may have a problem with your computer's port. Either way, get your Witch Doctor.

8. If all else fails and you're alone in the world, turn everything off and on, then try printing again. Believe it or not, that may solve the problem.

Good Witch Doctor Advice

Remember: Don't fool around with unplugging cables, or poking around inside your hardware while the machine is turned on or plugged in. (That is, unless you enjoy playing Russian Roulette.)

Reading Smoke Signals

The biggest problem you'll have when dealing with DOS commands is taming your own fingers. A typo, misplaced space, or backwards backslash can really mess things up. Here are some of the smoke signals to watch out for:

File cannot be copied onto itself

Thought you were going to copy that file, did you? Forgot to give it a new name? That's easy to do. Remember that if you want to keep a copy of a file in the same directory as the original, you must give the copy a unique name.

Invalid directory

You're telling DOS to show you the contents of a directory it doesn't see. Again, this problem is usually caused by badly placed fingers. Press F3 to see what you entered and then retype the command line as necessary.

Invalid parameter

You tried to do something DOS doesn't allow. Perhaps, for example, you tried to rename a file and in the same command move it to another directory. DOS won't go along.

PRINT queue is empty

You tried to use the DOS PRINT command, and DOS doesn't have anything to print. Specify a file after the PRINT command. Assuming that your printer is ready, that puppy should print — pronto.

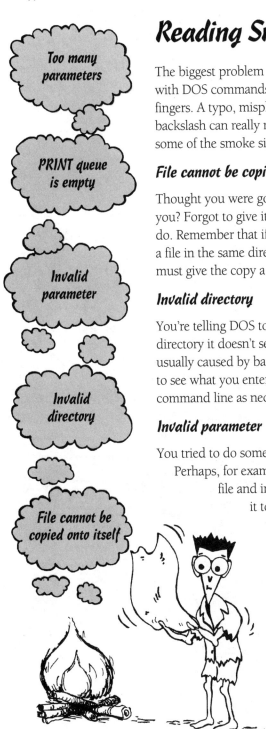

Too many parameters

PRINT queue is empty

Invalid parameter

Invalid directory

File cannot be copied onto itself

Oops! The natives don't look very happy. This appears to be the inside of their temple. One false move and you're diced chicken.

Too many parameters

DOS is telling you that you have too many of something in your command line — too many spaces, letters, directories, file names, or something else. Press F3 to see what you typed and fix the mistake.

You Know You're Really in Trouble When . . .

You accidentally delete files, and you have a version of DOS earlier than 5.0

Unless you have an undelete utility from another manufacturer (such as Norton), better start eating carrots to improve your memory. (Or is that eyesight? I can't remember.) Looks like you're going to be re-creating those files from scratch.

You typed an incorrect COPY command

Instead of copying all files from one directory to another, you told DOS to copy all files from one directory into a single file. This really isn't a catastrophe, just an inconvenience. Depending on the number of files you're copying and how long you have to wait for DOS to do its stuff, it could be a really big inconvenience. When DOS is finished doing your bidding, delete that waste-of-space file.

You accidentally renamed a file and gave it the same name you assigned to a Really Important File

Yup, you're right. You're in big trouble. That Really Important File is gone, gone, gone; you overwrote it with the renamed file. But you had a backup, right?

Chapter 8   Ready for Rescue

Paths through Peril

Now that you've come to the end of your journey, it's time to tackle the scariest trials and tribulations of all. It's pretty mysterious stuff, so (shhhhh!) please don't tell anyone that this is actually a chapter about memory — if people catch wind of it, you know they'll run. But it's not so bad really, not with the witch doctor by your side, or *S.O.S. For DOS* in your hands. And who knows, if you master this stuff, you might even be able to rescue yourself. Then think of the vast horizons before you and the untold stories of fame and glory. . . .

How Can I Be Out of Memory?

When you start using DOS with other application programs, you may get `Out of memory` errors. There's not much you can do about them right now.

An `Out of memory` error occurs because the programs or files you're working with are too big for the current operation to continue. Your computer just can't process anything else — there's no room. Here are a few things to try:

- Exit whatever program you're working with and get rid of any other programs you might be using that are eating up memory at the same time.

- You might be using a background program without even knowing it (for example TSRs). Things like day-planners, popup calendars or calculators, screen capture utilities, and modem programs that load automatically can eat up memory when you're not even aware of it.

- Reboot your computer to remove any additional programs (if the program loads automatically, have an expert check your AUTOEXEC.BAT file).

- Start the program again and see if things run more smoothly.

- Try working with a smaller data file.

- See if the program has an option that allows you to load it "light."

- Ask someone in tech support to run DOS's MEMMAKER memory-management utility on your hard drive to free up more space.

Techie Term

TSR is an acronym for terminate-and-stay-resident, which is a kind of program that continues to run (in the background) while you work with other things. An example is an alarm clock that beeps at you when you have an appointment.

How Can 4MB of RAM Be "Not Enough Memory?"

Poison: Your computer has plenty of memory. But the program you're trying to use says that it requires 580K of memory and only 556K is available. What about the other 4MB of chips in your machine? Why can't the program use those?

Oh no! Some type of trance. No telling where they'll be taking you now. This could be the beginning of the end.

Antidote: You just bumped into the *640K Barrier*, which most everyone does at one time or another. Welcome to the club — you'll learn the secret handshake later. In the meantime, you don't need *more* memory to solve the problem; you just need to *optimize* what you already have.

Note: For supremely detailed, no-nonsense explanations of different types of memory — conventional, extended, expanded, and upper — consult *DOS For Dummies.*

Before you start hacking up your configuration files, make sure that you have the following:

➡ A boot disk (a System Disk or Startup Disk)

➡ Current copies of your AUTOEXEC.BAT and CONFIG.SYS files

➡ A couple hours to spend digging your way out of trouble if (when?) things go awry

Depending on which version of DOS you're using, the quest for memory nirvana can range from anxiety provoking to challenging to expensive. Here's how things shake out:

DOS 4 and earlier: These versions of DOS don't offer any tools that will help solve your problem. Third-party memory programs such as 386Max, QEMM, and NETRoom may help, but only if you have a 386 or better machine.

If you own a 286 machine, seriously consider upgrading to DOS 6.2. It lets DOS load into high memory. If you own an XT computer, swallow hard and buy a new 486 computer. Sorry, there's nothing else I can do for you.

DOS 5: If you have a 286 or better machine, DOS 5 offers some tools to help address your memory problems. Use the EDIT command to get into your CONFIG.SYS file and look for these two lines

```
DEVICE=C:\DOS\HIMEM.SYS
DOS=HIGH
```

The two lines may not be next to each other, and they may look a little differently than they do here. If they're missing, type them in. Substitute the name of your DOS directory in the DEVICE command if it's different from the one in the example. Save the file and exit EDIT. Restart your machine and try the "problem" program again. If the error persists, read the next section.

Note: You must restart the computer before your memory changes take effect.

If the two lines are already in CONFIG.SYS — or if adding them doesn't solve your problem — you need your witch doctor. Although you have some useful memory tools available to you through DOS 5, it takes an expert to do the job right.

Protected Mode Problems

Poison: When you try to start a program, your computer says something about another program already using *protected mode*. *Note:* You'll only see this error message if you're using a 386 or better machine.

Antidote: Your program is complaining because only one application at a time can use protected mode, and some other bossy piece of software is using it right now.

The most likely cause of the error is a line in your CONFIG.SYS file. Use EDIT to open the file. Then look for a reference to EMM386.EXE. The statement will look something like

```
DEVICE=C:\DOS\EMM386.EXE
```

followed by a lot of arcane comments. To see whether this line is what's causing your program's headaches, do the following:

1. Type **REM** in front of the line. REM tells DOS to ignore the line

2. Restart your computer.

3. Try the program again.

If the problem isn't solved, something weird may be happening. Call your witch doctor.

Finding Out What's Loaded Where

Poison: Some drivers are supposed to be in upper memory, but how do you know for sure?

Antidote: MEM, your window on the computer's world, gives you the exact scoop.

MEM is only available in DOS 5 and 6. If you have a previous version of DOS, you need a third-party program such as Manifest, the Norton Utilities, or PC Tools to find out what's loaded where.

At the DOS prompt, type

```
MEM /C/P
```

Your screen will quake under powerful columns of raw memory data. When you catch your breath (yawn), look for programs with number entries in the High column on the right side of the display. They're "loaded high."

If a program is listed in the Conventional section, it's taking up your precious 640K base memory. It could be a candidate for loading high. Before doing anything, though, consult your Witch Doctor or a serious reference book, such as *PC World DOS 6 Handbook* (1993, IDG).

Techie Term

To meet the schizophrenic goals of technical advancement and backward compatibility, Intel (the processor people) came up with something called *protected mode*. It gives your computer the bells and whistles of the 1990s, while retaining precise compatibility with the 1981 "good old days." Ultimately, hardware and software will advance and this won't matter any more.

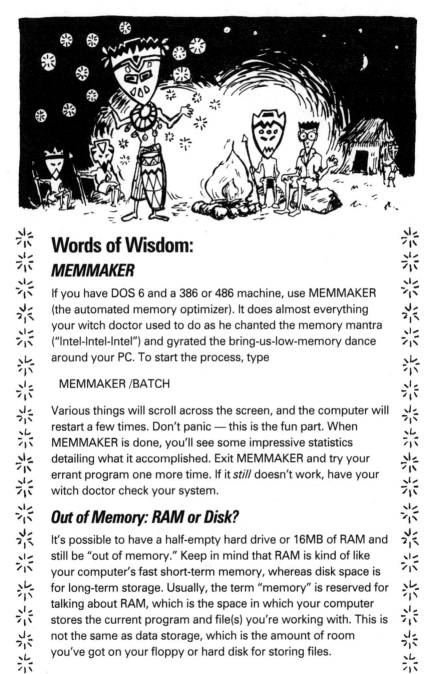

Words of Wisdom:
MEMMAKER

If you have DOS 6 and a 386 or 486 machine, use MEMMAKER (the automated memory optimizer). It does almost everything your witch doctor used to do as he chanted the memory mantra ("Intel-Intel-Intel") and gyrated the bring-us-low-memory dance around your PC. To start the process, type

    MEMMAKER /BATCH

Various things will scroll across the screen, and the computer will restart a few times. Don't panic — this is the fun part. When MEMMAKER is done, you'll see some impressive statistics detailing what it accomplished. Exit MEMMAKER and try your errant program one more time. If it *still* doesn't work, have your witch doctor check your system.

Out of Memory: RAM or Disk?

It's possible to have a half-empty hard drive or 16MB of RAM and still be "out of memory." Keep in mind that RAM is kind of like your computer's fast short-term memory, whereas disk space is for long-term storage. Usually, the term "memory" is reserved for talking about RAM, which is the space in which your computer stores the current program and file(s) you're working with. This is not the same as data storage, which is the amount of room you've got on your floppy or hard disk for storing files.

Starting High, Ending Low

Poison: Despite your best DEVICEHIGH or LOADHIGH instructions, some of your device drivers end up in base (640K) memory.

Antidote: This problem is caused by the peculiar way DOS loads programs into upper memory. If a program can't load into upper memory, it "falls down" into conventional memory.

With DOS 5, fixing things probably requires a witch doctor. The tweaking and optimizing has to be done by hand — and the hand needs to be an experienced, knowledgeable one. (If you want to get some knowledge for your hands, see *PC World DOS 6 Handbook* for excellent information on configuring system memory.)

If you've upgraded to DOS 6, go ahead and run MEMMAKER (see "How Can 4MB of RAM Be 'Not Enough Memory?'" earlier in this chapter for instructions).

If you've already done the MEMMAKER thing and still aren't happy, call the witch doctor and bake some brownies as an offering.

MEMMAKER Mangled Me

Poison: You ran MEMMAKER, and now several programs are on strike, one is seriously injured, and your mouse seems dead.

Antidote: Don't worry — for once, resolving the crisis is relatively easy.

If DOS isn't working right, restart the computer and press F5 when you see

```
Starting MS DOS . . .
```

Pressing F5 tells DOS to temporarily ignore both your CONFIG.SYS and AUTOEXEC.BAT files.

At the DOS prompt, type **MEMMAKER /UNDO** and watch the fun. MEMMAKER quickly removes the changes it made to your AUTOEXEC.BAT and CONFIG.SYS files. When DOS is finished, restart your machine. Things should be back to normal (well, at least as normal as things get with your computer).

RAM Disks and Why You Should Avoid Them

Poison: A coworker said you'd get more speed from your computer if you set up a RAM disk.

Antidote: Depending on the situation, your coworker could be right. Depending on the situation, though, he could flap his arms and fly to the moon, too.

Unless you have more than 16MB of RAM, stay away — *far* away — from RAM disks. Even if you *do* have that much memory, you can find better ways to invest it. SmartDrive and Windows make better use of extra RAM than a RAM disk, and they do it automatically. With a RAM disk, *you're* responsible for figuring out how to work things.

If that bit of advice didn't dissuade you from trying a RAM disk, and you want to know how to proceed, type **HELP RAMDISK** at the DOS prompt or consult your witch doctor. Don't ask me for help — you know what I'll say.

Techie Term

What's a *RAM disk*? It takes some of your expensive RAM memory and tricks DOS into believing that the RAM memory is a cheap disk drive. Yeah, right. If that sounds like a chewing-gum style kludge to you, you're on the right track.

How to Make a System Configuration Backup

Backing up your data is vital, but having a copy of your system configuration is important, too. The DOS command MSD (the nerd patrol's electronic equivalent of LSD) makes backing up your system configuration so easy that you'll actually do it.

Note: MSD (Microsoft System Diagnostics) is included with DOS 5 and 6 and all versions of Windows.

At the DOS prompt, type

```
MSD /F C:\INFO.MSD
```

This command creates the file INFO.MSD in your root directory.

Copy INFO.MSD to a floppy disk and store the copy with your backups. It's also a good idea to print a copy of the file and keep it near your computer.

When your witch doctor makes a service call and off-handedly asks whether you know your CMOS RAM settings (or something equally incomprehensible), whip out your file. Your witch doctor will be pleased (perhaps even perplexed and amazed).

For more information on MSD, please see Chapter 6.

Why You Should Be Kind to Your Witch Doctor

Witch doctors have a tough life. They come when something is broken, they're under the gun because you want it fixed *now*, and they sometimes have to deliver bad news. Consequently, they take a lot of abuse. To make your witch doctor's life a little easier consider the following advice:

- Don't blame him for your problems
- Remember that behind the funky mask, he's human, too (although I've met some possible exceptions)
- Be nice while he's there
- Don't yell, scream, or swear at the witch doctor
- No hitting. No biting. No throwing things. Period.
- Thank him when he's done

Of these, the last is probably the most important. Kindness and sincere thanks goes far with witch doctors. Home-baked cookies go further.

Besides, you can expect to pay from $35 to $120 (or more) per hour for a professional witch doctor. So, treat the poor guy with some respect, especially if you are getting good advice free of charge!

A snap of a witch doctor finger, and you come back to life. Oh my goodness, it is a monument — a sort of Easter-Island-like thing in your honor. How embarrassing. What flattery. Do these things really have bodies underground? But no time to check . . .

Expanding your Extended Memory (Or Is That Vice-Versa?)

Poison: MEM says that you have plenty of extended memory, but your program wants expanded memory.

Antidote: This problem requires a change to your CONFIG.SYS file — specifically, a change to the EMM386.EXE line.

Warning: Moments like these are why God invented witch doctors. Unless you're feeling hopelessly overconfident, consult your witch doctor before attempting this trick.

EMM386.EXE does double duty. It manages upper memory space (where things are loaded "high"), but its real goal in life is to convert extended memory into expanded memory.

EMM386.EXE works only on 386 or better machines. The 286 computers require special memory hardware to create expanded memory, and 8088 machines require a miracle.

To "create" expanded memory, begin by EDITing your CONFIG.SYS file. Look for a line that begins like this:

```
DEVICE=EMM386.EXE
```

If you see any parameters (like I=B000-B7FF) after the line, stop before it's too late and let your witch doctor handle this task. If you don't see any parameters, though, you can just type **RAM** at the end of the line. Save the file, leave EDIT, and restart your computer.

Next, type **MEM** and press Enter. If everything worked, MEM will report that you have 256K (or so) of expanded memory. Try your program again — is it happy? If not, (you guessed it!) call your witch doctor.

All of this time, they were only trying to help you get home again. You aren't the first traveler who has lost his way. How wonderful. And the witch doctor escorts you to the ship in his own sacred canoe.

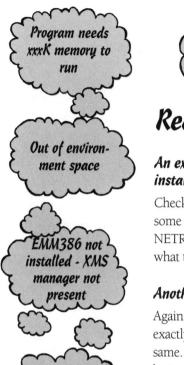

Program needs xxxK memory to run

Out of environment space

EMM386 not installed - XMS manager not present

Another protected mode program is running

An extended memory manager is already installed

Unrecognized command in CONFIG.SYS line x

Reading Smoke Signals

An extended memory manager is already installed

Check your CONFIG.SYS file for remnants of some other memory manager, such as QEMM, NETROOM, or 386MAX. If you're not sure what to look for, call the witch doctor.

Another protected mode program is running

Again, the message you see may not be worded exactly like this one, but the meaning is the same. The program you're trying to use wants to be in charge of protected mode, and some other bossy routine (probably EMM386.EXE) got there first. If the program is important to your life, call your witch doctor for a consultation on the best way to make it happy.

EMM386 not installed - XMS manager not present

This message sounds daunting, but it's actually pretty straightforward. For some reason, your HIMEM.SYS file (the "XMS driver") didn't load correctly. Find out why (see Chapter 1 for help with startup problems) and restart the machine.

The MS-DOS extended-memory manager, HIMEM, now automatically tests your system's memory when you start your system. This test identifies bad memory chips.

Out of environment space

Check your CONFIG.SYS file for a line that starts with the word SHELL. If you don't see one (which you probably won't), add the line

```
SHELL=COMMAND.COM /E:1024 /P
```

If the line's already in your file, increase the number after the /E to 2048.

Program needs xxxK memory to run

You won't see this exact error message — different programs have different ways of telling you that they need more memory. Optimizing your RAM may get your software running again. See the section "How Can 4MB of RAM Be 'Not Enough Memory'" for details.

Unrecognized command in CONFIG.SYS line x

If you see this message after a bout of memory optimizing, check your work. You probably mistyped a DEVICE or DEVICEHIGH statement. Otherwise, see Chapter 1 for more help.

You Know You're in Trouble When . . .

You added a SHELL statement to your CONFIG.SYS file, and now your computer can't get to DOS

This problem is only serious if you don't have a boot disk (such as your system disk). If that's the case, grab a witch doctor and beg for mercy.

Otherwise, insert your handy disk, restart the machine, and check the SHELL statement — chances are you'll find a typo in it.

MEMMAKER restarted your computer, but DOS didn't come up

Something didn't appreciate what MEMMAKER did to it. If you're feeling adventurous, get out your boot disk and restart the computer manually. Issue the command MEMMAKER /UNDO and see whether it restores your AUTOEXEC.BAT and CONFIG.SYS files. Or, if you're not feeling like Indiana Jones of the Computer World, call your witch doctor.

Oh heavens! Pirates in the distance, fast approaching
over the horizon. There's no time to waste. No time
to return to the island. Quickly, the witch doctor
has to hop aboard and travel with you to who
knows where . . . .

"Where are we headed?" you ask the captain,
with a small degree of apprehension. And
with the slyest of grins, he responds,
"Well, of course, we'll be
fast on our way now to a
land called Windows
Island . . ."

Epilogue

Oh, the stories you'll have to tell when this experience is over. They'll be boring grandchildren for generations to come. Twenty years from now, your DOS-wrestling feats will seem incredible. When multimedia, neural networks, and virtual reality fall by the wayside, all to be replaced by a brand of technology that we can now only imagine.

But there will always be witch doctors.

And there will always be those of us who feel stranded — cast away — by the rapid pace of it all, thrown into some kind of high-tech rat race with time. Sometimes, it's by choice, but too often all of this technology is imposed upon us. And in a sea of company procedure, policy, and politics, we are somehow left alone. Yes, set adrift in a sea of technology, with the human element distinctly no where to be found.

Take heart, though, because things have a way of coming around again. The pendulum swings this way and that. But it always comes back again. This week you'll be learning WordPerfect, and next week it'll be Excel. Tomorrow, who knows? But this much is for certain: There will always be folks who are willing to help each other — through it all.

An S.O.S. book may get you through this time, but don't worry, you'll find your own witch doctors. In the meantime, I've gathered together some advice from some of the best that we were able to track down. Sure, it's kind of general and philosophical, and it may not seem to relate to your problems much right now; but you'd be surprised. These are the secrets that every good witch doctor abides by. Study them. Learn to feel them, live them, breathe them.

There are at least a few of you out there who someday are going to be witch doctors, too. (Don't laugh; I'm not kidding.)

When Should You Call the Witch Doctor?

This is a personal decision. The range of choices runs from anytime to never. Take your pick. I'd say that it's safe to say that when you've run out of possibilities of your own for solving a problem, it's probably a good time to start.

Beyond that, think about the costs and benefits. State-of-the-art advice can be very expensive, and free advice can turn out to be very expensive, too. The most important thing you can do is become a proactive learner of the technology that confronts you. Apparently, you are, or you wouldn't be here. So, congratulations. I think you're on the right track.

So, What Do the Scrolls Mean?

I thought you'd ask. Here's what all of those hints were about in the DOS Island journey. Again, study them. A little troubleshooting theory isn't going to kill you.

Isolate the problem

Isolating the problem means finding what's *really* wrong. Many times, the surface symptom ("I just turned it on and it said 'Non-system disk or disk error.' Is my hard drive gone?") may or may not be the ultimate problem ("Hey! Who left this floppy disk in my computer?"). The trick to troubleshooting is finding and fixing *problems*, not *symptoms*. It's a process. One step and then another. Change one thing, try again. Pick a spot and troubleshoot in one direction.

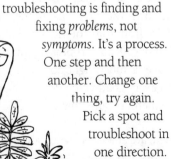

Isolate the problem and then solve it. One trick is to follow the power source. Follow the path of electricity. Follow the path of information. Rule out possible causes each step along the way.

Start Over and Try Again

The simplest case is: Turn it off. Wait a few seconds. Turn it back on. And try again. You would be amazed how may times this works. Who cares why. It just does.

When you have a problem. Go back to the beginnning. Retrace your steps. Things may not be as they had seemed when you first got into the mess.

Always Have a Backup

There's an old computer saying that goes like this: "There are two kinds of people in the world: those whose hard drives have failed on them and those whose haven't — yet." It's a real gem, isn't it? The saying is very true (everyone who's lost a drive is sagely nodding right now). If you're one of the lucky ones whose drive is still running, *now* is the time to learn about backups. Start today, right now, this minute — before it's too late.

Many application programs have an "autosave" feature which helps when you're deeply focused on "creating" and kinda-sorta forgot to save that document you just worked on all morning. If you've got this option, use it! Startup disks are something else you just can't have enough of. You should have at least one (preferably two) System Survival Disks handy at all times. Back up your passwords, too. If you're working with password-protected files, seal your password in an envelope and give it to your boss or other trusted coworker.

The simplest data backups involve copying things to floppy disks as you create them. For example, when you finish a document in your word processor, take a second and use the Save As command (or whatever it is in your particular package) to put a copy on a diskette. Save the original on the hard drive. To make the data *much* safer, take the disk home with you each night and bring it back the following day. Backups don't do much good if they're sitting next to the computer while the building burns down around them.

More complex and larger backups usually require extra accessories for your computer. The most common item is a tape backup system. It's common to use more than one tape when you back up this way. With two tapes, you'd use Tape #1 this week and Tape #2 next week. The third week, go back to Tape #1. This way, you always have a backup for your backup.

Backups are funny things. If you never need them, dealing with them seems like more of a pain than it's worth. When the time comes (and it will), you'll look like a hero. Put some serious time and effort into designing a backup system for your computer. If your PC is your lifeblood, find a witch doctor to get you set up. Remember that you're doing this for yourself — a backup is personal insurance that *will* pay off; the only question is when.

Know How to Undo Things

So here you are: something bad happened and you want to go back in time to the point before whatever-it-is went wrong. In short, you want to *undo* the crisis. Undo is one of those techno-philosophical concepts that keeps many nerds going at 3 a.m. and many Chinese restaurants flush with late-night business.

Depending on your situation, "undo" can have many forms. Conceptually, you're trying to reverse or otherwise bail out of a bad situation. Here are some ideas to get you out of whatever dire straights you've gotten yourself into:

- **Keep a current backup.** A good backup is the ultimate "undo."

- **Quit without saving.** Almost every program known to mankind has an almost neurotic desire to save your changes. What if you don't *want* to save them? Close the file or quit the program. When it asks if you want to save those all-important changes, say no. Voilà! You're right back to where you started.

- **Try Undo.** The Undo command traditionally lets you escape the consequences of whatever heinous software crime you've committed, but ONLY your most recent one. Multiple heinous software crimes are beyond the forgiving capacities of Undo; seek solace from Quit without Saving.

- **Escape, Ctrl-C, and Ctrl-Break.** These are DOS-level tricks (although Escape often works in application programs too!). If you typed **FORMAT C:** just to see what it looked like sitting there on the command line and are now too terrified to move, press any of these keys. They tell DOS to ignore what's on the command line (Escape) or stop whatever it's trying to do right now (Ctrl-C or Ctrl-Break). By the way, they're in order by strength. Often, Ctrl-Break will get you out of a bind that the other two won't seem to affect.

- **Beware of programs that make changes for you.** Many installation routines "help" you by posting changes to your CONFIG.SYS and AUTOEXEC.BAT files (and WIN.INI for Windows programs). Granted, they usually warn you of what they're about to do, but it's still not the same as a qualified witch doctor inserting the same changes. If things don't work right after the automated surgery, look for the backup copies of these files.

- **Look for automatic .BAK files.** Some programs (such as Microsoft Word) automatically make backup files for you.

Don't Make Assumptions

Believe it or not, this is what separates decent troubleshooters from Great Witch Doctors. If you master it, it will have the same effect on your computing future. When you're trying to resolve something, watch out for your assumptions. Like blinders that limit your vision, they can send you off on wild-goose chases, snipe hunts, Congressional fact-finding junkets, and other wastes of time. Incorrect assumptions can even *prevent* you from finding the correct answer. How do you avoid this?

- Don't get focused on "the answer" too soon. Sometimes a problem appears that you've dealt with before. You immediately implement your tried-and-true solution, which doesn't work this time. After spending time and effort chasing an assumed problem, you've still got the real problem left to solve. Using previous experience is vital, but always leave your mind open to new twists on old plots.

🖝 Separate obvious symptoms from hidden problems. This goes back to good troubleshooting technique.

🖝 Don't assume it's *really* a problem. Many, many "problems" are solved by just turning the stupid machine off and on again. Try it. Keep in mind that the average 386 is doing a few million things *per second*. If it runs without a hitch for one minute, it's done *several hundred million* consecutive things right. If it screws up once in a while, who could blame it? Restart and then give it a chance to try again.

🖝 Look for the right things. If you're having an "I've lost something" crisis, don't assume you're looking in the right place. Make sure you've got the right *file* in the right *directory* on the right *disk*.

🖝 Don't assume any one step is working. Think through the process step by step. Things you skipped because you assumed them to be correct can be your downfall. Check and then check again.

🖝 Don't assume the blame yet; it may not be your fault. When something in your computer does the electronic equivalent of going "ping," it's perfectly normal (if not factually correct) to blurt out "I broke it. I killed it. It's all my fault." Many times, *you* didn't break it. It just broke. Don't jump on yourself too quickly.

If you *did* do it, learn from the experience. Keep your perspective. These things are never *that* tragic — really. Don't verbally berate yourself into a high blood pressure prescription; it's just not worth it.

Don't Panic

"Format complete," the screen sadistically chirps. A thick veil lifts from your consciousness and you wonder, "Format of *what* is complete? Was I *formatting* something?!?" Your stress level begins an inexorable climb as you remember all those silly questions the computer rather unexpectedly asked you a few minutes ago (the ones like "All data will be erased. OK to proceed?" and the almighty "Are you sure?"). Did they really *mean* something? Visions flash before your eyes: spreadsheets predicting the financial future of your world, Pulitzer prize-winning justification memos, that super-cool jet fighter game with the high score in your name. Your eyes grow wide and the index finger on your left hand begins to involuntarily twitch.

This is *panic*. And panic-stricken people do not operate computers very well.

Bury what I'm about to say deep in your subconscious where it can fight its way to the surface when your brain hits the panic button: *get up and get away*. Put a little sign on the computer that says "having a bad hair day" and walk out of there for a few minutes. Get all the emotion out of your system and regain logical control before you even think about sitting down at your computer again. This *will* be hard, but you'll thank me later.

When it's time for your moment like this, remember that madly thrashing around trying to "fix" whatever crisis you're having will probably do more damage than the crisis itself entails. Almost any problem can be solved, provided a logical, rational mind is at the helm. If you think the problem is that big, call someone before you try anything. Panic throws everything out of proportion, making even the smallest of problems look like a disaster. Just go somewhere and settle down. When you're approximating normalcy again, have another look at your computer.

Think First

Don't jump wholeheartedly into the first possible solution; think about what you're doing. Sit back and *think* about the problem you want to solve. Thinking costs nothing yet can save mondo amounts of time, effort, and psychological wear and tear. Think first before you issue that FORMAT command, before you copy that file, before you turn off your machine. Being in too much of a hurry now can cost you hours of grief later.

Write It Down

Witch Doctors are part of another realm, thus error messages that look like gibberish to us might be useful to them (of course, it might be gibberish to them too, but they just don't want to tell us). Being rescued doesn't mean you couldn't have done it yourself. In fact, if you play your cards right, you *can* do it yourself next time. If you get yourself in a jam, write down the problem and how you got out of it. Then, whenever you get stuck, consult your list to see if you had the same problem before. If so, great. You can look at the steps you took last time and fix things yourself.

If not, that's okay, too. Just write down how you fix the problem this time so that next time you'll know what to do.

Be specific; don't approximate error messages. If it beeped, write down any patterns (long-short-short). If you tried solutions, write down what you did and in what order (the order is as important as what you did). Write down how you fixed it this time. Write down all the steps you went through when you created something. Write down how you answered queries. Write down what you didn't do. Very often these notes will save your neck later.

Don't Move

When you're troubleshooting, one thing often leads to another, which leads to another, and you keep digging further as you chase the elusive problem.

So many times you find a problem and think "Hey — this one'll be easy." Ultimately, you find that you've landed the Queen Mother of All Iceberg Problems. Somewhere along the way, it begins to exceed your ability; the problem begins to win. You'll raise your eyes from the morass of unplugged cables, strewn manuals, and scribbled notes. Your brain will desperately whisper, "I'm over my head. I think I'm in trouble."

Moments like this can be great learning experiences. They can also be the last moments of your computer's useful life on the planet. Knowing when to call for help is a most valuable skill in computer troubleshooting. It saves wear and tear on you, your computer, and your witch doctor.

Once you reach this point, frantically resist the urge to try "just one more thing." Witch doctors often perform miracles but (equally as often) are seriously impaired by the "last thing" their acolyte tried. If a problem is serious enough that you've given every bit of skill and daring you possess chasing it to the ground, it's also important enough to make you swallow any remaining pride and speak the words "Help me; help my computer."

Once you've given up, don't go back. If you get a brainstorm and you're *positive* this will solve the problem, write down your thoughts and sit on your hands. Discuss your idea with the witch doctor. Don't attempt the resolution again. You might be taking that last step which separates you from the digital disaster.

Don't Be Afraid

I heard someone say once that people just need to take responsibility where their computers are concerned. Keep a positive, nonintimidated attitude. Basically, be a proactive user. Take charge of your PC. Take ownership. Divide and conquer. . . .

Know more about it than it knows about you. They're not as smart as some people think, you know. So they can add up a bunch of six-digit numbers fast — big deal.

Your computer is dead weight without your intervention. Make the best of it.

Index

❏ YES!

Please keep me informed about IDG's World of Computer Knowledge. Send me the latest IDG Books catalog.